THE GIFT OF TRUTH ITSELF

Avatar Adi Da Samraj
Adi Da Samrajashram, 2008

THE GIFT OF TRUTH ITSELF

THE EVER-LIVING MEANS WHEREBY EVERYONE CAN REALIZE TRUTH, OR PERFECT HAPPINESS

SELECTIONS FROM *THE ALETHEON*,
THE FINAL MASTERWORK OF
AVATAR ADI DA SAMRAJ

AN **ADIDAM**™ INTRODUCTORY TEXT

THE DAWN HORSE PRESS
MIDDLETOWN, CALIFORNIA

NOTE TO THE READER

All who study the Reality-Way Given by Avatar Adi Da Samraj or take up its practice should remember that they are responding to a Call to become responsible for themselves. They should understand that they, not Avatar Adi Da Samraj or others, are responsible for any decision they make or action they take in the course of their lives of study or practice.

The devotional, Spiritual, functional, practical, relational, and cultural practices and disciplines referred to in this book are appropriate and natural practices that are voluntarily and progressively adopted by members of the practicing congregations of Adidam Ruchiradam (as appropriate to the personal circumstance of each individual). Although anyone may find these practices useful and beneficial, they are not presented as advice or recommendations to the general reader or to anyone who is not a member of one of the practicing congregations of Adidam Ruchiradam. And nothing in this book is intended as a diagnosis, prescription, or recommended treatment or cure for any specific "problem", whether medical, emotional, psychological, social, or Spiritual. One should apply a particular program of treatment, prevention, cure, or general health only in consultation with a licensed physician, medical practitioner, or other qualified professional.

The Gift of Truth Itself is formally authorized for publication by the Ruchira Sannyasin Order of Adidam Ruchiradam. (The Ruchira Sannyasin Order of Adidam Ruchiradam is the senior cultural authority within the formal gathering of formally acknowledged devotees of His Divine Presence, Avatar Adi Da Samraj.)

Produced by The Dawn Horse Press, a division of
The Divine Avataric Holy Institution of Global Adidam Ruchiradam.

International Standard Book Number:
978-1-57097-333-8

Library of Congress Control Number:
2013939623

CONTENTS

CAPITALIZATION, UNDERLINING, QUOTATION MARKS: Avatar Adi Da Samraj uses capitalization, underlining, and quotation marks to distinguish between ordinary speech (which describes the conditionally manifested reality) and speech that describes the Non-conditional Reality. With the use of capitalization and under-lining, Avatar Adi Da expresses a different view of the world, in which Truth and the terms that relate to that Greater Reality are given more significance than the language of the separate ego and the conventional world. With quotation marks, Avatar Adi Da often communicates that some ordinary term, commonly pre-sumed to point to something real, is, in Reality, pointing to an illusion. He also uses quotation marks to point to a specific, technical meaning He intends. ■

ABOUT THE COVER

Throughout His life, Avatar Adi Da Samraj focused intensively on developing both literary and artistic means of communicating the True Nature of Reality. He approached the creation of His literary and artistic works as a process of Revealing What Reality Is and how Its True Nature can be Realized.

The image on the cover is a photograph He created in 1999.

Examples of the artwork of Avatar Adi Da Samraj, together with discussions of His artwork and His own statements about it, may be seen online at

www.daplastique.com

Avatar Adi Da Samraj
Adi Da Samrajashram, 2008

INTRODUCTION

By Brian O'Mahony

How do we know what is really and undeniably True, or Truth Itself? The starting point for Avatar Adi Da's examination of Truth Itself is that everyone already has a tacit (or intuitive) sense of the Truth—because the Truth, or the true nature of Reality, is the native State of everyone and everything. In His words, Truth is "always already the case"—no matter what happens in life. Yet the true nature of Reality remains only an intuition, rather than a full enjoyment or realization, in almost everyone's case. Avatar Adi Da points out that fullest <u>Realization</u> of Truth (or Reality) is "absolutely uncommon", and most people are unaware of even the possibility of such Realization. In *The Gift of Truth Itself*, Avatar Adi Da explains why this is so, and He offers the great process by which anyone and everyone can actually Realize the Truth, thereby Realizing Liberation from all suffering and limitation.

The Gift of Truth Itself draws together selections from *The Aletheon**—Avatar Adi Da's final summary of His entire Teaching-Revelation. This *Aletheon* compilation begins with a concise consideration of the cultural, religious, and social forces that have shaped Western humanity's presumptions about Truth and Reality. These influences have now become globally extended, in both East and West, thereby tending more and more to underlie all common religious and secular ideas about the nature of Reality. Avatar Adi Da reveals how these pervasive thought-patterns not only hide the nature of Reality but even actively work against its Realization. He gives a penetrating description of how the

---

* *Aletheon* (pronounced a-LAY-thee-on) comes from "aletheia", the Greek word for "truth".

11

typical human developmental process from childhood to adulthood produces false notions of Reality, Truth, and God. And He shows how it is only by understanding and transcending the limitations of this cultural and social inheritance, and of human egoity itself, that Truth can be Realized. Through His radical examination of these presumptions and limitations, Avatar Adi Da enables us to inspect the paradigms that rule our lives—and to understand how they can be gone beyond.

After considering what obstructs and limits humankind, Avatar Adi Da goes on to describe what has traditionally served the process of Realization. He discusses the esoteric tradition of real Spiritual practice and the essential function of the Spiritual Master—also called Guru, or Adept-Realizer—at the source of every true Spiritual Way. He describes His own Spiritual Work as an extension of that great esoteric tradition—and, indeed, as its perfect fulfillment and completion.

In the end, and in fact throughout this book, Avatar Adi Da makes a great offering—the opportunity to enter into the utterly Liberating relationship to Him. This relationship is available to anyone, regardless of cultural background, now and forever into the future.

Reality and egoity

Avatar Adi Da Samraj describes Reality (the true nature of everything seen and unseen) as the Indivisible Oneness of Consciousness and Light, or "Conscious Light":

If you examine "objects" more and more profoundly, sooner or later you get down just to Energy Itself, Light Itself. Similarly, if you go within, beyond all the outward functions, you get to Consciousness. Those are the two "extremes" of the One Reality. But they are not, in fact, separate realities—they are only presumed to be such, from your "point of view". And this is the nature (or pattern) of un-Enlightenment.

Energy Is the Radiance of Consciousness Itself. Consciousness Is the Source-Position of Radiance Itself. Self-Existing and Self-Radiant* Consciousness Is Love-Bliss Itself— Unconditional Feeling, Radiance.

When there is this Awakening, it is obvious. In every moment, Natively, Inherently, It Is simply the Divine Conscious Light— the Infinite, Dimensionless, Uncaused, Eternal "Brightness" of Being (Itself).

—Spoken Communications from Avatar Adi Da Samraj
March 29, 1998

In *The Gift of Truth Itself,* Avatar Adi Da Samraj also uses other words and phrases to describe the One Great Reality—"Truth", "Real God", "the Divine", and "the 'Bright'". He makes it clear that Reality Itself—Divine Existence, or Perfect Happiness—is the birthright of all beings, the Prior Condition of each and every one.

And, yet, Adi Da points out, this glorious Reality remains mostly hidden to human awareness—intuited and sometimes glimpsed, but never fully Realized. Avatar Adi Da explains why this is so in His unique Teaching about the activity of the ego, and the life of apparent divorce from Reality that results from that ego-activity.

Avatar Adi Da writes that the sense of separate "self", or ego-"I", is first established in early childhood and becomes the pole around which the entire life revolves. He points out that this sense of a "self", separate from all "others", is not the natural state. It is an illusion—in truth, there is no separate "self". The sense that there is such a "self" is produced by an active recoil of the entire being in the face of the vulnerability of the born condition. Avatar Adi Da calls that recoil "the 'self'-contraction".

---

* Avatar Adi Da uses the terms "Self-Existing" and "Self-Radiant" to indicate the two fundamental aspects of Reality Itself: Existence (or Being, or Consciousness) Itself, and Radiance (or Energy, or Light) Itself.

The activity of self-contraction patterns all the physical, emotional, mental, and psychic dimensions of human existence. From this sense and activity of separation stem all false notions about Reality. An apparent world of separate beings and things is seen from an apparently separate point of awareness called "I". Everyone is vulnerable—aware that, no matter how good or seemingly secure life might be at the best of times, the death of "I" can and will happen sooner or later.

To seek relief from the certainty of mortality, human beings look to be distracted and consoled. Some presume and hope that there is a God who created all of this and who offers an afterlife where "I" will continue and even realize eternal happiness. Others affirm and seek for a transcendent Reality that they can become one with, even in this life, while persisting as "I". Some notice the illusory nature of "I" and work to expunge it. Many others simply cope, believing that the material world is all there is, and that when you die, that is the end. These presumptions are reflected in the many secular, religious, and Spiritual paths developed by humankind.

But, as Avatar Adi Da masterfully demonstrates in *The Gift of Truth Itself*, all such presumptions ultimately hide the true nature of Reality, because they revolve around the preservation, satisfaction, liberation, annihilation, or salvation of the illusory separate "self". The limitation inherent in the presumption that we each exist as the ego-"I" remains at the core of all experience. Therefore, Avatar Adi Da says that it is only in the <u>transcending</u> of the ego (or the separate "self") that the true nature of Reality can be known, experienced, and Realized.

The Intervention of the Avatar

How can such transcending be accomplished? Since it requires going beyond self, there is no <u>self</u>-applied effort or technique that can lead to that Realization. All such efforts of human seeking, high and low, ultimately fail to relieve the sense of separate "self" and the limited and mortal life it produces. Thus, Truth Itself can be Realized only as a Gift—not as something attained by the separate "self".

Avatar Adi Da's entire Life and Work is the bringing of just such a Gift. He Reveals that Reality Itself directly "intervenes", or brings the Gift of a process in which the root-activity that is ego-"I" can be dissolved, forgotten, and replaced by the Knowing and Enjoying of Reality as It Is, Prior to egoity. Mysteriously and remarkably, this intervention of Reality occurs in the form of the Avatar:

Something in the Super-Physics of the universe makes it possible for the Divine Conscious Light to Avatarically Incarnate as an apparent human individual, for the Purpose of Bringing others into the Sphere of Divinely Enlightened Existence. —Avatar Adi Da Samraj, pp. 104–5

"Avatar" is originally a Sanskrit word meaning "One who has crossed down". A unique Intervention is indicated—not merely an individual who has attained some degree of enlightenment by Spiritual effort, or even a reincarnating Master, but a Direct Appearance, in physical form, of the One Supreme Reality, or Divine Conscious Light.

There are many prophetic references to the appearance of the Avatar in the Spiritual traditions of the world. Aldous Huxley speaks of this tradition in *The Perennial Philosophy*, where he refers to Reality, or the Divine, by the Greek term "Logos":

The Logos passes out of eternity into time for no other purpose than to assist the beings, whose bodily form he takes, to pass out of time into eternity. If the Avatar's appearance upon the stage of history is enormously important, this is due to the fact that by his teaching he points out, and by his being a channel of grace and divine power he actually is, the means by which human beings may transcend the limitations of history. . . .

That men and women may be thus instructed and helped, the godhead assumes the form of an ordinary human being, who has to earn deliverance and enlightenment in the way that is prescribed by the divine Nature of Things—namely, by charity, by a total dying to self and a total, one-pointed awareness. Thus enlightened, the Avatar can reveal the way of enlightenment to others and help them actually to become what they already potentially are. . . . And, of course, the eternity which transforms us into Ourselves is not the experience of mere persistence after bodily death. There will be no experience of timeless Reality then, unless there is the same or a similar knowledge within the world of time and matter. By precept and example, the Avatar teaches that this transforming knowledge is possible, that all sentient beings are called to it, and that, sooner or later, in one way or another, all must finally come to it.*

Nine months before Avatar Adi Da's birth, the great Indian sage Upasani Baba made a remarkable utterance. He prophesied that an Avatar would "soon be born in a European country". "He will be all-powerful," Upasani declared, "and bear down everything before him."† Upasani Baba's prophecy was not premeditated—according to the records, it was a spontaneous outburst. He was foretelling the appearance of One who would bring a unique clarification and completeness to all the cultures of the past, both East and West. Similar prophecies of the liberating appearance of a final or completing Prophet, God-Man, Buddha, or Avatar, exist from ancient times.

Avatar Adi Da Samraj is the fulfillment of these prophecies. His Appearance in the world is the Manifestation of the Divine Reality Itself via a human form—a form capable

---

* Aldous Huxley, *The Perennial Philosophy*, 1st Harper Colophon ed. (New York: Harper & Row, 1970), 51, 56.

† Speaking in February 1939 to the head of one of the most important Hindu monastic orders (the Shankaracharya of Jyotir Math). In the early twentieth century, "European" was often used by Indian speakers of English to mean "Western". See B. V. Narasimha Swami and S. Subbarao, *Sage of Sakuri*, 4th ed. (Bombay: Shri B. T. Wagh, 1966), 190–91, 204.

of communicating, speaking, acting, writing, and relating to human beings in ways we can understand and respond to. His appearance in human time shifted the pattern of existence at its core, such that beings can directly respond to the Divine Reality Itself, even via a personal form. His incarnation in human form has enabled immediate and real access to the "Reality-State", the true Context in which everything and everyone is appearing.

Avatar Adi Da said that it took countless incarnations to make His conjunction with a human form possible. Throughout time, great Realizers of different degrees have appeared and helped humankind in the context of various traditions and cultures—but this completing Divine Avataric Incarnation is without boundaries or "tribe". His Avataric impulse to Bless and Awaken beings encompasses and embraces everyone and everything, in all times and places. And His Work is Eternal. As He says, His "Visit" was unique— it does not need to be repeated, because It will never end.

I am not merely "the Spiritual Master for this time".

I Am the egoless Absolute Person of Reality Itself— Coincident with this time, and Consequential forever.

—Avatar Adi Da Samraj
The Aletheon

Avatar Adi Da's devotees are those who recognize Him as That One, the Perfect Manifestation of Truth, Reality, or the Divine in this world. But such recognition of Adi Da as Avatar is not a matter for belief. In fact, Avatar Adi Da cautions that there is no virtue in relating to Him on the basis of mere belief. The Truth of Who He Is is something that becomes directly self-evident—in other words, incontrovertibly true, beyond the sense of "personal knowledge" and prior to conceptual mind. The process whereby someone comes to know and deeply trust Avatar Adi Da and His Work is unique to each one.

The Great Offering of Truth Itself

Having Appeared as the completing Avataric Intervention, Avatar Adi Da invites any and all beings to enter into relationship with Him for the purpose of perfect Liberation:

I Communicate My Own "Bright" Divine Self-Nature, Self-Condition, and Self-State to you, thereby Effecting a "radical" (or "at-the-root") transformation in the disposition of your body-mind-"self".* *And, then (over time), I Magnify the effectiveness of that disposition many times, such that the entire Process of Divine Enlightenment can, potentially, take place even in a single lifetime—or (at least) be dramatically advanced in one lifetime, if not completely fulfilled.*

—Avatar Adi Da Samraj, p. 106

In *The Gift of Truth Itself,* Avatar Adi Da Samraj makes this great offering—to bring about Reality-Realization in all who recognize Him and most deeply resort to Him in devotion. In essence, as He demonstrated from the very beginnings of His Work in the world, He only offers "a relationship, not a technique". The process of Reality-Realization requires a radical transformation of the body-mind-"self" of the practitioner, a transformation that is effected and magnified and quickened through the Power of His Blessing-Grace. If you enter into the devotional relationship to Him, He says, "the Divine Process begins to duplicate Itself in your case". This is the Reality-Way of Adidam He has Given, and which everyone is invited to consider and embrace.

Beyond His offering of the Reality-Realizing process to those who become His devotees, Adi Da Samraj also extends

---

* The English word "radical" is derived from the Latin "radix", meaning "root" (or "irreducible", "fundamental", or "relating to the origin"). With the compound term "body-mind-'self'", Avatar Adi Da is communicating that each human being is a complex of fundamental faculties, including body, mind, emotion, and breath. This complex is typically presumed to be a separate "self" or ego-"I".

His Avataric Blessing and Regard to all of humanity, regardless of religious and cultural background and affiliation. Humankind as a whole deeply needs to be converted from its signs of global strife and terrible suffering, which stem from the unconscious patterning of separately presumed selves and separately presumed group-identities. The Truth that is Prior to all ego-presumption must be awakened at the core, the literal "egolessness" or "prior unity" that is native to human beings and to even any being or thing in this world. Avatar Adi Da Calls for a transformation of global culture on this basis, in His seminal book *Not-Two Is Peace*. And He Works constantly, in both the Transcendental and Spiritual* dimensions, to bring about this transformation.

I Am Looking for men and women who will live free of every kind of seeking, attendant only to the consciousness of universal prior unity, who will constantly devote themselves to the responsible cooperative management of individual and collective human life in the Indivisible Form and Logic of Reality Itself, rather than the egoic and separative form and "difference"-bound logic of egoity and illusion.

Such men and women are the unexploitable human presence of Reality Itself.

—Avatar Adi Da Samraj
Not-Two Is Peace

What could be of more import in this necessary global transformation than to become a conscious participant in what everyone intuitively knows to be fundamental, True, and Real—and to do so by devoting oneself to the process of its fullest Realization?

May all who read this book receive the Gift of Truth Itself from Avatar Adi Da Samraj and respond to His unique Offering. ■

---

* Avatar Adi Da uses "Transcendental" to refer to the Consciousness dimension of Reality and "Spiritual" to refer to the Energy dimension of Reality.

The Life and Work of Avatar Adi Da Samraj and His Final Teaching-Revelation in *The Aletheon*

By Megan Anderson

T*he Aletheon*—the masterwork from which the selections in this present text are drawn—is not exactly a book. It is, rather, a kind of "universe" of exposition and Revelation. It is the representative and ever-living communication of a legacy of Divine service and Blessing, covering fundamental aspects of human experience of which most people are not even aware. Adi Da derived the name for His final work from the Greek word for truth, "aletheia"—and it is indeed (in the nuance the Greek term implies) the perfect unveiling of what has been heretofore unknown, or concealed.

The words from that "universe" that you will encounter in this text did not come out of philosophical research or argumentation in the scholarly arena, nor from someone who is simply a "writer-philosopher" in any ordinary sense. These words come to you directly from one who lived only—and consciously so—for the sake of enabling people to know the Great Reality and Truth of existence. At the end of Avatar Adi Da's Lifetime, this final Expression emerged, one that (perhaps more than any other single communication He made) truly embodies His life's mission.

As the previous pages have described, the history of Avatar Adi Da's Lifetime is the consummation of the ancient understanding of "Avatar": the breakthrough of the Great Eternal Reality into the ordinary world, through the mysterious process of intentionally assuming physical incarnation. This

Avataric nature is demonstrated in the story of Avatar Adi Da's Lifetime—both through His innate sign of outshining all apparent obstructions to the Realization of Reality and Truth and through His movement to embrace everyone and everything universally, even in the face of such apparent obstructions. The events that unfolded between Avatar Adi Da's human birth in November 1939 and His physical passing in November 2008 are thus, in some sense, the best evidence of the Eternal Truth and Presence He reveals in *The Aletheon*, and also in this book.*

Avatar Adi Da's apparently ordinary birth in November 1939, in Jamaica, New York, was His initial embrace of human life. But, for His first few years, He experienced only free resonance with the "Bright" State of Reality and Truth that had brought Him, as Avatar, into conjunction with the world in the first place. It was only in His third year that a deep awareness of the pains and limited presumptions experienced by others drew Him to spontaneously assume a limited persona in the likeness of others, as a means to communicate Reality and Truth in the world. In the years that followed, Adi Da engaged a remarkable ordeal of embracing and outshining the principal presumptions of human life (separate self, separate others and world, and separate "God") in His own experience. This lasted until September 1970, when the "Bright" Truth that was His very nature, from birth and even before, fully re-asserted itself.

In these first thirty years of His life, Adi Da Samraj embraced and outshined experience in all its highs and all its lows: family, religion, love, pleasure-seeking, intellectual pursuits, Spiritual practice and the aspiration for Truth, extraordinary mystical experience, and profound states of awareness and freedom. It was during these years that much of the understandings and principles presented in Parts One

* For Avatar Adi Da's full Spiritual Autobiography, please see *The Knee of Listening* (Middletown, CA: The Dawn Horse Press, 2004).

22

and Two of this book were first consciously experienced and expressed by Adi Da Samraj, as a result of His utter embrace of the global human culture into which He had appeared as Avatar.

After His Re-Awakening to His Native State of "Brightness" in 1970, a new form of service to beings began to unfold for Avatar Adi Da. His experience was no longer of a consciously created "separate self"—as which He had lived since early childhood—but rather He began to experience a kind of work, or "meditation", that was extended into the field of all selves, all forms of conscious life, though registered directly within His own body and mind. And so He continued the process of "embrace and outshining", but now in a universal field. This became a thirty-year ordeal of Teaching and Spiritual Blessing, in direct human relation to those who appeared around Him, attracted by the Communication of Reality and Truth that He embodied—and simultaneously taking place in relation to everything and everyone.

In these second thirty years of His life, Avatar Adi Da exhaustively considered and elaborated a Way of life and Spiritual practice that is fully resonant with Reality and Truth. He re-examined everything He had uncovered in His own early life, but now in relation to others, communicating fully about the Realization of Reality in the context of human life—and about all the ways that humanity dodges or denies Reality-Truth by living in presumed separation from It. Avatar Adi Da also took those who became His devotees through an extraordinarily comprehensive and profound examination of the religious and Spiritual paths of East and West. Altogether, He worked to free everyone from their ordinary ego-patterning, and also from fascination with all the kinds of extraordinary experience that can arise in the course of Spiritual life.

Through all of this, He demonstrated—face to face—the deeply transformative Blessings of the relationship to a human Master who is the embodiment of Reality and Truth. The ecstatic communications of Part Three of this text, which stand utterly "outside the box" of any presumption of separate self or world, were all spoken or written in the context of this profound service to those committed to the Awakening of Reality and Truth in His Company. Part Three is therefore a kind of unique "window" into the living relationship with Avatar Adi Da that He is offering to you and everyone. It is a living demonstration of "outshining", spoken directly to your heart.

In April 2000, the years of Avatar Adi Da's universal ordeal to Teach and Bless by means of embracing others came to fullness in an event of complete "outshining", in which His body appeared to come close to death. Afterward, Adi Da's ability to relate to others as they appeared to be (in their suffering and limitation) essentially fell away, and His sign from that time became more and more a pure and simple expression of His "Bright" State of Reality and Truth, as in His earliest childhood. He began to focus in the non-conceptual communication of Reality and Truth, creating an extraordinary body of visual art, and He also established the final forms of His Spiritual Teaching and His Address to the entire world-culture.

Avatar Adi Da began creating *The Aletheon* in September 2006, two years before His physical passing, as a consummate and free communication of this final stance of "outshining". He incorporated writings and discourses He had given throughout the years of His Work to Teach others, and He created many writings and new statements as well. He conformed all of this—in its flow of argument, its language, and its sheer monumentality—to His pure Revelation of His State. The Avatar had completed His Work of engagement in the world of apparent "others", and now spoke only as Himself, as He always Is, even before and after His human Lifetime. Avatar Adi Da finalized *The Aletheon* on the morning of the day He passed from His body, in November 2008, by writing its subtitle in His own hand: "The Divine Avataric Self-Revelation of His Divine Presence, Avatar Adi Da Samraj". That culminating gesture can be understood as a sign that His Work in human form was complete. When He relinquished the body that He had embraced in order to make His Self-Revelation, Adi Da retired to the "Place" of the Avatar's Eternal State. That State is the Reality to which He Calls everyone. And it is that State which Avatar Adi Da Gracefully Offers to Awaken in all who respond at heart to His Gifts. ▪

Avatar Adi Da Samraj
Adi Da Samrajashram, 2008

PROLOGUE

Conscious Light Is Always Already The Case

Conscious Light
Is Always Already The Case

Conscious Light Is Reality Itself.

Conscious Light Is Truth Itself.

Conscious Light Is What <u>Is</u>.

Conscious Light Is Always Already The Case.

Conscious Light Is
Self-Evidently Divine,
Absolute,
All-Inclusive,
All-Transcending,
All-Love-Bliss,
Non-exclusionary,
Non-"different".

Conscious Light is not the Case
merely under certain conditions.

Conscious Light Is Always Already The Case—
no matter what the conditions,
whether or not there <u>are</u> any conditions.

Reality Itself,
or Truth Itself,
or Real (Acausal) God
is not "within" you.

Reality Itself,
or Truth Itself,
or Real (Acausal) God
Is Consciousness Itself,
Which Is Always Already The Case.

There is no "you" about it.

Your presumption of separateness
is a result of the relinquishment
of the Self-Awareness
of the Position of Consciousness Itself.

When That Position is re-Established,
there is no dilemma.

T ruth is Most Prior (or Eternal) Freedom and Humor.
Truth is the Only Perfect Refuge.
Truth Is That Which, when "Known" (or fully Realized), Sets you Free.

Reality Is What *Is* (no matter what arises or changes or passes away).
If Reality (Itself) is Self-"Located" (and, Thus, "Known", or fully Realized), Truth (Itself) is "Known" (or fully Realized)—and you are (Thus and Thereby) Set Free.

AVATAR ADI DA SAMRAJ

PART ONE

WHAT IS REAL AND WHAT IS TRUE?

TRUTH AND REALITY
CAN BE NEITHER PROVEN
NOR DISPROVEN

In this opening statement, Avatar Adi Da calls us to approach His arguments in Part One with openness—specifically, a willingness to be released of inherited beliefs and ideas. He also expresses the compassionate intention that underlies His criticism of human culture.

1.

I do not "believe" <u>anything</u>.

The Prior renunciation (or intrinsic transcending) of <u>all</u> mere belief is the basis on which I have <u>always</u> lived—and the basis on which I have Done <u>all</u> of My Divine Avataric Work.

There are <u>no</u> mere ideas that must—or even should—be accepted <u>absolutely</u>.

Indeed, there are <u>no</u> mere ideas that are acceptable <u>As</u> Truth.

2.

Truth Itself cannot be proven.
Truth Itself is not in doubt.
Therefore, neither can Truth Itself be disproven.

Reality Itself cannot be disproven—nor can Reality Itself be proven.
Reality Itself is Intrinsically and tacitly Self-Evident.

3.

I have much to Say of a critical nature relative to egoity (as it manifests both individually and collectively), and relative to all the "stuff" of humanity and its mere ideas.

Nevertheless, My Criticism is Spoken in a positive Disposition.

There is no harm intended in My Criticism.

Therefore, My Criticism Cures the heart, and Cures the life—but by the Means of Truth Itself, or Reality Itself.

TRUTH IS NOT
A MERE SOCIAL GOSPEL

In this first major essay, Avatar Adi Da discusses the pervasive cultural influence of conventional religious teachings, using the historical role of Christianity in the West as a primary example. Becoming aware of this cultural inheritance (and its limitations) is essential to the process of discovering the Truth of Reality.

The Influence of Christian Concepts
On Western Culture

If you grew up in the Western (and predominantly Christian) cultural sphere, you are perhaps influenced by the "New Testament" more than by any other "religious" book. Even if you are not very familiar with the "New Testament", you have (nevertheless) been impressed, over the years, with certain conventions of "religious" presumption of which the "New Testament" is the source. The conceptions associated with the traditional interpretation of the "New Testament" are not only part of the "religious" teaching of Christian churches, but part of Western culture in general. Through your schooling, through your childhood "religious" training, and through the influence of those with whom you were associated as a child—even though they might not have spoken of "religion"—you have been greatly influenced by these conceptions, some of which are directly communicated in the "New Testament" itself and others of which are simply traditions that are, by extension, associated with "New Testament religion".

Everyone is dominated, to one or another degree, by conceptions of life that have their origin in exoteric* "religious" culture. Even though scientism (or scientific materialism) is tending to displace exoteric "religion" as a way of "knowing", exoteric "religion" still tends to be the basis for present-day morality and social conceptions. In fact, exoteric "religion" has traditionally always been associated with moral and social conceptions. Thus, if you are, by birth, a Westerner, and even if you were not brought up as a Christian, you have, since your birth, been exposed to propaganda that is, at least in its origins, both conventionally "religious" and specifically Christian. And the basic intention of all such conventionally "religious" propaganda has been to convince you—and, thus, the collective of everyone—that certain kinds of behaviors are appropriate and other kinds of behaviors are not appropriate.

Every present-day legal system—and even the entire body of social contracts by which people are related in their daily lives—has its justification in the tradition of exoteric "religion".

Reducing Religion
To A Kind of Humanism

Exoteric "religion" is primarily a communication that intends to bring political and social order to the public "world". Exoteric "religion" is primarily a social gospel. Esoteric ecstatics, on the other hand, are very difficult to control—in the usual (conventional) sense. It is virtually impossible, for example, to interest ecstatics in being socially productive for its own sake. Ecstatics generally value the practice of being civil in relation to other people—but it

---

* Avatar Adi Da uses the term "exoteric" to describe conventional religious practice that focuses in beliefs about an objective Deity. He contrasts exoteric practices with "esoteric" practice that participates in the process of Realizing the Truth of Reality.

is very difficult to get them to labor in factories and bureaucratic business organizations merely for the sake of "worldly" success, or, otherwise, to get them excited about the mundane purposes of a great State! Therefore, exoteric "religion" tends to eliminate all aspects of "religious" communication that suggest anything but how to be a productive and positive social personality. To reinforce these qualities—and even to suppress ecstatic qualities—is the guiding purpose of exoteric "religion".

Even though Christianity is, in its origins, an esoteric movement, it was reduced to an exclusively exoteric "religion" as it became more expansive and eventually achieved the status of the "official" (or politically enforced) State-"religion" of the West. Christianity thus became an exoteric (or conventionally social) institution, and it reduced the teaching of Jesus of Galilee* to a social gospel. The result is that now everybody commonly assumes that, since the "New Testament" is, historically, the primary "religious" influence in the Western "world", "religion" is supposed to be a social gospel, and Jesus must (therefore) have taught a merely social gospel.

In this "late-time" (or "dark" epoch)†—when even all cultures are being moved toward the way-of-"knowing" represented by scientific materialism, and all cultures are losing their sacred basis for order, and are tending to be dominated (more and more) by the forces of political materialism—the interpreters of the "religious" texts of cultures other than the culture of the West are, likewise, moving more and more toward an exoteric interpretation of esoteric teachings. India,

---

* Some scholars and archaeologists have called into question the traditional identification of the town of Nazareth as the place where Jesus spent the early years of his life. However, the New Testament Gospels clearly associate Jesus with the region of Galilee. Therefore, Avatar Adi Da uses the reference "Jesus of Galilee" (rather than "Jesus of Nazareth").

† Avatar Adi Da uses the terms "late-time" and "'dark' epoch" to describe the present era—in which doubt of God, Truth, or Reality (or anything at all beyond mortal existence) is more and more pervading the entire world, and the self-interest of the separate individual is more and more regarded to be the ultimate principle of life.

for example, has, since the later nineteenth century, been undergoing a kind of renaissance of Hinduism. The Bhagavad Gita is a principal text in this movement in India—and one of the dominant tendencies of current interpretation conceives the teaching of the Bhagavad Gita as a kind of social gospel. In other words, the Bhagavad Gita is, now, publicly interpreted as a source of exoteric instruction about how to live the way of "good works", rather than the mystically interiorized esoteric way of life that is characteristic of traditional Indian Spirituality.

Thus, the Bhagavad Gita—which, in its origins, is an esoteric teaching about Spiritual and Transcendental Realization—is being used, more and more, to support a cultural, political, and social movement of an exoteric kind. In this manner of "religious" interpretation within the Indian cultural sphere, the Bhagavad Gita is being interpreted (and, thus, used) in a manner that is very similar to the traditional exoteric interpretation (and even the earliest exoteric inventing) of the "New Testament" in the West.

To the degree that they are "religious" at all, people all over the Earth now commonly conceive of "religion" as a kind of social message. It is commonly presumed that "religion" is reducible to a kind of humanism—even a kind of atheistic humanism (or a humanity-centered, rather than Deity-centered, positive social life)—or, at least, that "religion" is totally compatible with the "world"-oriented, humanity-oriented, socially-oriented propaganda of the time.

You are constantly "TV'd" into the presumption that you are born for the sake of being born, that you are born into this "world" for the sake of this "world". The presumption conveyed by TV (or the pervasive conventional mentality) is that life is an end-in-itself, and one is supposed to be enthusiastically involved with things of this "world". Luckily (so the usual person presumes), there is science, technology, and a certain amount of freedom—and, therefore, it is possible to be rightly enthusiastic about conditional existence. People have a great deal of hope that, during their lifetime, they will achieve more and more pleasure, leisure, and fulfillment of their human functions. All over the Earth now, everyone is being propagandized into social consciousness, the positive social gospel that is now coming from the realms of scientific materialism and its political arms around the "world". If current secularizing trends continue, sacred texts such as the "New Testament" and the Bhagavad Gita are in danger of becoming obsolete. If that occurs, then positive and enthusiastic social principles or ideals will, more and more, be communicated all over the Earth completely independent of any kind of "religious authority"—and, of course, entirely removed from any kind of esoteric teachings.

Truth Is About
Transcending self and World

However, it is important to understand that the teachers and the teachings that are at the origins of the true scriptures of humankind (and of the various cultural movements associated with those scriptures) are not of an exoteric nature. Those teachers and teachings were not about the social gospel which the State has traditionally looked to "religion" to generate. If you understand the real fundamental (and esoteric) teaching underlying the "New Testament" and other traditional scriptures, you will see that those scriptures are not exoteric social gospels at all. Rather, those scriptures are esoteric communications about transcending the egoic "self" and the "world" and Realizing True Communion (and, ultimately, egoless Self-Identification) with the Divine Self-Condition.

The social gospel—and the socially positive "point of view" that the State wants to generate and to support by various means—is not at all about transcending the "world" by Realizing the Divine Self-Nature, Self-Condition, and Self-State of Reality Itself. Likewise, that social gospel is not about transcending the apparently individual "self" by "self"-sacrifice in the Divine Self-Nature, Self-Condition, and Self-State of Reality Itself. The State is purposed to have people transcend their otherwise egoic (or even "Godward" and ecstatic) inclinations by means of productive work. In other words, the State likes the ideal of individuals who are "transcending themselves" by being devoted to the purposes of the State. The State generally tolerates the large-scale communication of "religion" only if the message is exoteric (or socially oriented). The ideal must lead the common individual to be a "good" social personality—doing his or her job, being honest, not making trouble, not creating disorder, not being lazy.

The State is not interested in any kind of teaching about transcending the egoic "self" and the "world" in Communion with the Divine Self-Nature, Self-Condition, and Self-State of Reality Itself. The State is not at all in that business, nor does the State like such teachings. The State—and its "official" cult of the time—did not like Jesus of Galilee. One could say that present-day "official" Christianity also does not like Jesus of Galilee—and for the same reason. The "official" Church has never liked the ecstatic Jesus, who taught everyone to be an ecstatic, like himself, and so to transcend the selfish "self" and the "world" (or the "flesh") in the Spiritual Divine. Nobody has ever really liked Jesus of Galilee, except those people who are able to respond to the Truth in Spiritual terms. Such people have always been relatively rare.

If you are truly Transcendentally Spiritually Awakened, then you <u>intrinsically</u> transcend the (apparently separate) ego-"self" and the (apparently "objective") "world"—in every moment. Even if the machine of the body-mind-complex is active in one or another manner—as it inevitably is, because it is born in the frame of space and time—no action need bind you in any manner whatsoever, if you will rightly understand the nature of the body-mind-"self" and the "world", and if you will practice life on the basis of that right understanding.

This is the logic of the teaching of Jesus of Galilee, and (indeed) the logic of the teaching of <u>all</u> the great Spiritual Adepts. The great Spiritual Adepts do not come into the "world" merely to guarantee social order, nor can their teachings be rightly reduced to a social gospel. The teachings of Jesus of Galilee are not reducible to the "Ten Commandments" and some sort of socially positive emotion that is called "love".

The conception of "works"—or performing action for the sake of becoming holy, "sinless", deserving of heaven after death, happiness, fullness, success while alive—is discussed in the "New Testament", just as it is discussed in the Bhagavad Gita and other traditional scriptures. If you understand the esotericism represented by such figures as Jesus and Krishna (or by the essential teaching communicated by the texts in which such figures are the principal characters), you will see that no traditional scripture recommends the way of the social-personality-for-its-own-sake. In other words, no true traditional scripture is a merely social gospel, or a gospel that (ultimately) is merely a justification for a positive social personality whose "salvation" lies in "works", or the cultivation of positive behaviors. In fact, the traditional scriptures (such as the "New Testament" and the Bhagavad Gita) all teach the <u>transcending</u> of bondage to "works", the <u>transcending</u> of the necessity (and the "effects") of all ordinary action.

THE WESTERN PROHIBITION AGAINST HIGHER KNOWLEDGE AND REALIZATION VERSUS THE EASTERN ADVOCACY OF HIGHER KNOWLEDGE AND REALIZATION

Extending the argument of the previous essay, Avatar Adi Da Samraj contrasts the characteristic dispositions of the West and the East relative to the Realization of Truth.

The Western Taboo Against Oneness With The Divine

I n Western (or Occidental) literature, mythology, and "religious" legends, stories, and doctrines, there is a characteristic and persistent tendency to associate a negative connotation or result with the quest for higher "knowledge" (and, altogether, with the process of esoteric initiation, esoteric "knowledge", and esoteric Realization). In the traditional Western (or Occidental) literatures, there is (characteristically) a "penalty" for those who approach the Divine too closely, or who even seek to Realize Oneness with the Divine. Indeed, the tendency to confine human existence and human potential to the mundane, the material, the physical, the social, and all that is merely exoteric is the principal characteristic of the Western mind, all of Western culture, all of Western "religion", and all that characterizes the Western (or the "Westernizing") and the "modern" (or the "modernizing") influence and tendency.

In the ancient Jewish story of the Garden of Eden, Adam and Eve are penalized for taking the fruit of the Tree that would give them the unique "knowledge" that would put them on a par with "God". In the myths of the ancient Greeks, Icarus and Prometheus are punished for "getting too close" to the sun and to fire—and, when Bellerophon rides his winged horse, Pegasus, up to the dwelling place of the gods, he is thrown down because he presumed he could attain the status of the gods. Likewise, Jesus of Galilee is, according to tradition, said to have been crucified for claiming Oneness with the Divine. As these famous examples (along with many other examples) indicate, the traditions of the West (or traditions that, otherwise, characterize what can be identified as the Western, or Occidental, mentality) are typically associated with the prohibition against higher (and, altogether, esoteric) "knowledge" and Realization. Therefore, there is a basic presumption in the traditional West (and in the characteristically Western mind) that one must neither own too much nor "know" too much—but, coincidently, the traditional West (and the characteristically Western mind) is possessed by a persistent fascination with owning and "knowing", and even a kind of lust to own everything and to "know" all.

The Eastern Glorification of Esoteric Realization Versus The Western Fear of Esoteric Realization

In the characteristically Eastern (or Oriental) traditions, the unique (or defining) characteristic is the opposite of the unique (or defining) characteristic of the Western (or Occidental) traditions. Therefore, in the typical Eastern (or characteristically Oriental) traditions, the stories, the myths, and the "religious" legends and doctrines are unambiguous about the praising, the glorifying, the seeking, and the attaining of higher (and, altogether, esoteric) "knowledge" and Realization.

The characteristic tendency (and ambivalence) of the Western mind shows itself not only in literature, mythology, and "religion", but also in the basic Western (and characteristically "modern") inclination toward materialism (including scientific and political materialism), which is an enterprise of conventional "knowledge" (and of "worldly" power) that dogmatically eschews and systematically excludes all that is esoteric (or all that is metaphysical, or Spiritual, or Transcendental, or Divine). Therefore, the West (and all that is characteristically "modern") is characterized by ambivalence (and even suppressiveness) relative to higher (and, altogether, esoteric) "knowledge" and Realization, and (otherwise) by a clear preference for exoteric and materialistic "knowledge". It can even be said that Western culture (and all of "Westernized", or "modern", civilization) is founded not only on materialism but on an actual and persistent (and gravely limiting) <u>fear</u> of higher (and, altogether, esoteric) "knowledge" and Realization.

By contrast, characteristically (and traditionally) Eastern (or typically Oriental) culture and civilization is associated with a positive and most profound orientation toward higher (and, altogether, esoteric) "knowledge" and Realization. Also, the typically Eastern (and typically Oriental) mind and orientation is characterized by far less interest in (or attachment to) material things than is (otherwise) seen in the West (and, altogether, in the "modern", or "Westernized", "world").

The Necessary Out-Growing
of Esophobia

I n short, the West (in and of itself) is "esophobic", or inherently afraid of What Transcends the conventionally "known" or "knowable"—whereas the East (in and of itself) is "esophilic", or inherently "self"-identified with all that is of a higher (or, otherwise, Transcendent) nature.

Therefore, the Out-Growing of the now universalized Western "esophobic" tendency, and its ambivalence, its materialistic revulsion, and its suppressiveness relative to the "esophilic" (and not merely Eastern, but Really Spiritual, Transcendental, and Self-Evidently Divine) Process of Self-Realizing the Self-Nature, Self-Condition, and Self-State of Reality Itself is the principal necessity for even all of humankind in this "late" (or "Westernized") time and in this "dark" (or "modern") epoch.

CHILD-MADE AWARENESS
OF REALITY

*In this excerpt from a longer talk, Avatar Adi Da locates the
origins of conventional religious ideas about "God" in the
natural childhood situation of dependence on one's parents.*

In general, discussions about "God" or "religion" tend to
be naively associated with the idea of the Power that is
"Other", or the One Who is "Other". This "God"-idea
corresponds to a rather childish (or even infantile) sense of
Reality. Children are not, in general, great metaphysicians or
great mystics! They have some very primitive kinds of
awareness, as well as some remarkable kinds of awareness
that adults tend to lose or dismiss. However, when children
communicate their sense of "God", they very often express a
feeling that has been dictated to them by their parents. They
naively describe Reality according to a child's psychology—
that child-made awareness of Reality which is not natively
associated with great, abstract propositions. It is not that
children are free of mind, and (therefore) their "religious" concepts are purer than those of adults. The "religious" concepts
to which a child can be sensitive and responsive are generally built upon the psychology of the childhood situation—
which is one of being dependent on a parent or parents,
particularly on the mother. The parent-child relationship—in
which the parent is a great, "experienced" person there to
protect the smaller, vulnerable person—provides the naive
basis for childish "religious" views and for what are commonly called "religious" views in general. In other words,

the notion that people have of "God"—apart from Real-God-Realization Itself*—tends to be a carryover, an extension of the childish situation. Therefore, "religion" tends to be regarded as a "solution" for a rather infantile "problem": the need to be protected, sustained, and made to feel that everything is all right and that everything is going to be all right, the need to feel that there is a superior "Other" in charge of everything.

When people communicate to their children about "God", they commonly speak of "God" as a kind of super-version of mommy-and-daddy. When people speak to one another about their earliest "religious" consciousness (and it is more a kind of conventionally acquired mental attitude than it is a matter of direct perception), they commonly talk to one another in terms of a child's model of Reality. However, to truly enter into the Process of Reality Itself, you must transcend the child's version of Reality. To become human, to be an adult, a mature human personality, you should have overcome that childish view.

---

* Avatar Adi Da uses the term "Real-God-Realization" to mean "the Realization of Truth Itself, or Reality Itself."

THE CHILDISH PRESUMPTION
OF "GOD-APART" AND
THE ADOLESCENT PRESUMPTION
OF "SEPARATE SELF"

Extending His discussion of the impact of early-life experience, Avatar Adi Da Samraj argues that the fundamental human presumptions about "God" and "self" are inevitably generated in the developmental course of childhood and adolescence—and the Realization of Truth requires the transcending of those limited presumptions.

1.

E verything a child does is a manifestation of one underlying presumption: dependence. When you are a child, the presumption of dependence is eminently realistic and useful. But it should be a temporary stage of psycho-physical life, in which one's functions are nurtured and developed in conventional ways. However, there is commonly a lag in the transition to adulthood, because of the shocks encountered in the immature attempts to function in the "world". Thus, to some degree, every adult lingers in the childhood presumption of dependence. And, insofar as adults are children, they seek to enlarge that personal presumption of dependence into a universal conception in the form of the "God-Cosmos-Parent" game—the game of dependence upon (and obedience to) That upon Which all depends. That childish aspect in each individual always seeks to verify the condition of dependence in forms of safety and relative unconsciousness. That childish demand in every adult human being is the principal origin of exoteric "religion". Exoteric "religion" is the search to be re-united, to "experience" the vital and emotional re-establishment of some imagined or felt condition (or state) of life that is previous to responsibility. It is the urge toward the parented, enclosed condition. This urge always seeks "experiences", beliefs, and immunities as a consolation for the primitive cognition of fear and vulnerability. And the "Way" enacted by such a motivation is principally a game of obedience to parent-like enormities.

2.

It is in childhood that the idea of "God-Apart", or "Reality-Beyond", is conceived. The sense of dependence initiates the growing sense of separate and separated "self" through the "experiential" theatre of growth. The intuition of the Whole, the One, is the ground of birth—but "growing up" is a conventional pattern of initiation in which the sense of "difference" is intensified. At the conventional level of the life-functions themselves, there is a need for such functional practical differentiation. However, in the plane of consciousness, the presumption of "difference" gives rise to an unnatural adventure of suffering and seeking-in-dilemma.

3.

The passage of childhood thus becomes the ground for the eventual conception of the mutually exclusive trinity of "God-Apart", "separate self", and "world-in-itself" (any "world", high or low). The drama implied in the added presumptions of "independent self" and "objective world" is generated at a later phase of life than childhood. The child barely comprehends the full force of implication inherent in the concepts of "ego" and "world-of-things". The child's principal concern is relative to the "God-Parent-Reality" (or That on Which all depends), and relative to his or her growing (but, as yet, not fully conscious) sense of separated "self"-existence. "Separate self" and "objective world" are yet hidden in unconsciousness for the child. The concepts of "separate self" and "objective world" are a later (and mysterious) comprehension of that which is (at first) only felt, not conceptualized, as fear and sorrow. Therefore, the child is always grasping for permanent security in a non-differentiated, un-born bliss, wherein the threats implied in life are forgotten and unknown. Re-union through obedience is the manner in which the living child learns in secret, while the life that grows the child through "experience" continually demonstrates the failure of all childish seeking.

4.

There must be a transition from childhood to maturity. That transition is commonly acknowledged as a stage in the psycho-physical development of the human being. It is called "adolescence". Like childhood, this stage also tends to be prolonged indefinitely—and, indeed, perhaps the major-ity of "civilized" human beings are occupied with the con-cerns of this transition most of their lives. The transitional stage of adolescence is marked by a sense of dilemma, just as the primal stage of childhood is marked by a sense of dependence. It is in this transitional stage that the quality of living one's existence <u>as</u> a dilemma is conceived. It is the dilemma imposed by the conventional presumption of sepa-rate, egoic, independent consciousness—and, thus, separa-tive habits and action. That presumption is (altogether) the inevitable inheritance from childhood—and its clear, per-sonal comprehension, felt over against the childish urge to dependence, is what initiates the ambivalent conflicts of the phase of adolescence.

5.

The dilemma of adolescence is a continual goad to dramatization. It is the drama of the double-bind of dependence-
versus-independence. Adolescence is the origin of cleverness
and, in general, of mind. What we conventionally call the
"conscious mind" is a strategic version of mind which is
always manufacturing motivations. And, in the adolescent,
these motivations (or desires) are mutually exclusive (or con-
tradictory). This is because the adolescent is always playing
with impulsive allegiance to two mutually exclusive principles:
dependence and independence. The early (or childhood)
condition yields the tendency to presume dependence—but
the conventional learning of childhood, as well as the inherent growth-pattern of the individual psycho-physical being,
yields (to the growing person) the equally powerful tendency to presume independence. The result is conventional
consciousness (or "conscious mind"), as opposed to the
unconsciousness of childhood—but that conventional consciousness is strategic in nature, and its foundation is
the conception of life-as-dilemma. Therefore, adolescence is
the origin of the great search in all adult human beings.
Adolescence is an eternally failed condition, an irrevocable
double-bind.

6.

By the time the child fully achieves the life-strategy of
obedience to That on Which all depends, he or she has
entered the phase of adolescence. At that point, the individual fully presumes the ego-"self" and the "world" as apparently independent (or "objective") dimensions, exclusive of
(or other than) the "Reality" that is the goal of all dependence. Therefore, the path of obedience, fully developed, is
already a path of dilemma, of conflict, of struggle with

"self"—as every "religious" person comes to understand through "experience". Truly, then, the "experiential" fruition of the life-strategy of childhood (or dependence) is fully demonstrated only in the advent of human adolescence.

7.

In adolescence, the separate, separated, and separative "self" is the motivating presumption behind the common suffering and the common heroism of humanity—both in life and in Spirit. The sense of permanently independent existence is the source of the dilemma that undermines the non-differentiated dependence of mere birth. In the adolescent, there is the unrelenting search for the success, "self"-fulfillment, unthreatened security, immunity, healing, extreme longevity, immortality, and ultimate salvation of the presumed ego-"I". The ego, "self", or "soul" is the primary presumption of the adolescent—just as "God-Apart", or That on Which all depends, is the primary presumption of the child. Therefore, in the usual human being, who is embedded in the adolescent conception of existence, the idea of "God" falls into doubt, or is chronically resisted. Thus, "sin" (or "missing the mark")* enters into the mind of adolescence. And the "world" becomes merely a scene of the adolescent drama in which even the very "stuff" of the "world" is viewed as a "problem", a principal warfare of opposites, and in which the manipulation of conditionally manifested things (rather than Realization of the Eternally Present Nature, Condition, State, Form, and Process of Reality Itself) becomes the hope of peace.

---

* The Greek word in the New Testament which was then translated into English as "sin" was "hamartia", originally an archery term meaning "missing the mark".

8.

There is a mature, real, and true phase of human life. Real and true human maturity is free of all childish things and free of all that is attained, acquired, and made in the adolescent adventures of conventional life. In that mature phase, the principle of separation is undermined by means of real "self"-understanding*—and the mutually exclusive trinity of "God", "self", and "world" is returned to the Condition of Truth Itself. In the maturity of human life, the "world" is not abandoned, nor is it lived as the scene of adolescent theatre, the adventure in dilemma. "God-Apart" occupies the child, and "separate self" occupies the adolescent—and both child and adolescent see the "world" only in terms of their own distinct limiting principle (or characteristic form of suffering). But, in the mature human being, the "world"— or the totality of all arising ("subjective" and "objective", high and low), not as an exclusive "reality" but in Truth—is primary. In the mature individual, the "world" is (potentially) apprehended as a modification of the Single, Indivisible, Absolute, Non-separate Reality—implying no "separate self" and no "outside God". For such a one, the Absolute Reality and the "world" are not "different". The Absolute Reality Is the Divine Nature, Condition, State, Form, and Process of all-and-All.† The Absolute Reality Includes all that is manifest, and all that is unmanifest—all universes, conditions, beings, states, and things, all that is "within" and all that is "without", all that is visible and all that is invisible, all that is "here" and all that is "there", all dimensions of space-time and All that is Prior to space-time.

---

* Avatar Adi Da uses the term "'self'-understanding" to mean the process of directly observing and transcending the activity of ego (or "self"-contraction).

† Avatar Adi Da Samraj uses the phrase "all-and-All" to describe the entirety of conditionally manifested existence, both as the sum of its parts ("all") and as a Totality altogether ("All").

55

9.

The mature phase of human life is not characterized by either unconscious dependence or the strategically conscious dilemma of dependence-independence. Rather, the mature phase of human life is the phase of relational participation (rather than childish dependence) and real human responsibility (rather than adolescent independence). As in childhood, there is no "problem"-based strategy at the "root" of the mature phase of life. Childhood is a realm of unconsciousness, whereas the mature person is freely conscious. Unlike the adolescent, the mature human being conceives no irreducible dilemma in life and conscious awareness.

10.

This mature phase of life requires, as its ongoing foundation, the (at least eventual) most fundamental understanding of the egoic "self". The separate and separative principle of independent "self", the strategies of mind and desires, the usual ego-possessed life of the avoidance of relationship,* the urges toward unconscious dependence and mechanical or wild independence, and all the mediocre solutions that temporarily balance or fulfill the extremes of "experience"— all of these must be obviated in most fundamental "self"-understanding. The mature (or responsible and truly conscious) phase of life is, thus, the origin of the real practice of life (or true action). And the mature phase of life, fully demonstrated, is characterized not by the usual "religious and Spiritual solutions", but by no-seeking, no-dilemma, no orientation toward the goal of any conceived or remembered state or condition. Only in the mature phase of life can you

---

* Avatar Adi Da uses the phrase "separate and separative" to describe the ego's activity of enforcing separate "self" (separateness) and its inclination to exist as a separate entity (separativeness). He also uses the phrase "avoidance of relationship" to describe and summarize this separative activity.

Realize the Perfectly Prior (and, thus, Always Present) Self-Nature, Self-Condition, and Self-State That <u>Is</u> Reality Itself. Only a human being thus free "Knows" conditionally manifested existence in (and <u>As</u>) the Self-Nature and Self-Condition and Self-State of the Real (and Intrinsically egoless, and Perfectly Acausal) Divine, Which is also the Process and Form and Light and Fullness of all the "worlds".

Avatar Adi Da's "Map" of the Seven Stages of Life

I n the preceding essay, Avatar Adi Da summarizes the process of early-life development and how it relates to conventional conceptions about Reality. In the following essay (and other readings in this book), Avatar Adi Da refers to the early-life process as "the first three stages" within His fully elaborated "map" (or schema) of seven potential stages of human development.

Taken together, the first six stages of Avatar Adi Da's schema account for all the fundamental orientations to life that have arisen in human history—including all the orientations to religious, Spiritual, and Transcendental practice. Avatar Adi Da's unique Revelation of the seventh stage of life is intrinsically egoless Realization of the Divine Conscious Light, transcending all previous human orientations and demonstrations.

The first three stages of life constitute the foundation of ordinary human adaptation—the bodily, emotional, and mental adaptation necessary for basic human survival and participation in human society. Every individual who lives to an adult age inevitably adapts (at least to a basic degree) to the first three stages of life. However, since the vast majority of human beings lack the guidance necessary to consciously participate in and complete this developmental process, fullest right adaptation within the first three stages is rarely the case. Religious traditions based fundamentally on beliefs and moral codes (without direct experience of the dimensions beyond the material world) belong to this foundation level of human development.

Only a rare few have moved into the esoteric (or more advanced) stages of life. The examples of history's yogis, saints, and sages show that there are profound Spiritual and Transcendental potentials beyond what is commonly realized at the foundation of human life.

The fourth stage of life is characterized by a deep sense of devotional and (in due course) Spiritual Communion with the Divine, felt to be a Great "Other" with Whom the being yearns for Union.

In the fifth stage of life, attention gravitates "Above" to the domain of subtle experience, seeking the states of blissful transport that are associated with the process of Spiritual ascent, and potentially culminating in a formless (though not permanent) Ecstasy.

The Realizer of the sixth stage of life is focused "Deep Within", in identification with Consciousness—by intentionally excluding awareness of (and involvement with) arising phenomena, whether the phenomena are of a gross (material) or subtle (energetic, emotional, and/or mental) nature.

Avatar Adi Da Samraj is the unique Divine Revealer of the seventh stage of life, and His Divine Blessing-Transmission is the unique means by which the seventh stage Realization will be Awakened in prepared individuals throughout future time.

In the seventh stage of life—which is Realized only in the context of most profound devotion to Avatar Adi Da Samraj and most profound renunciation of separate ego-existence—the fifth stage impulse to Realize the Divine as the Light "Above" and the sixth stage impulse to Realize the Divine as Consciousness "Deep Within" are both simultaneously, effortlessly, and permanently fulfilled, in the Perfect Love-Bliss-Fullness of Divine Enlightenment. In that supreme Awakening, Avatar Adi Da Samraj Himself is recognized and

(continued on next page)

Realized as the Source-"Brightness", the Single Divine Unity of Consciousness <u>and</u> Light—or Conscious Light Itself. Everything that arises is understood to be merely a modification of the One Divine "Brightness", the Conscious Light of Reality Itself, Which Is Avatar Adi Da's Divine State and Person.

As Avatar Adi Da says of the seventh stage Realization:

It is Inherently Free of any apparent implications, limitations, or binding power of phenomenal conditions. If no conditions arise to the notice, there is simply the Self-Existing and Self-Radiant Self-Nature, Self-Condition, and Self-State of Transcendental, Inherently Spiritual, Intrinsically egoless, and Self-Evidently Divine Being. Such Is Absolute (or Inherently Most Perfect) Realization of That about Which nothing sufficient can be said—and there is not Anyone, Anything, or Anywhere beyond It to be Realized.

—"God-Talk, Real-God-Realization,
Most Perfect Divine Self-Awakening,
and The Seven Possible Stages of Life",
The Aletheon

For Avatar Adi Da's summary description of the seven stages of life, please see Part Four of *The Aletheon*. ■

GOD AS THE CREATOR, GOD AS GOOD, AND GOD AS THE REAL

In this comprehensive essay, Avatar Adi Da lays bare the logic (and the inherent problems) of theistic belief—and also of atheistic "belief". He demonstrates the ultimate untenability of any system of thought that presumes separate "self" to be true.

The Dogma of Theism

Conventional "God-religion" originates in the state of mind that characterizes the first three stages of life. Thus, conventional "God-religion" is ego-based—and it serves the functional desire of the egoic (or phenomenal) "self" to be protected, nourished, pleasurized, and (ultimately) preserved.

The phenomenal "self", or egoic ("self"-centered) body-mind-complex, is the source of conventional "God-religion", as well as all of the other ordinary and extraordinary pursuits of born existence in the first six stages of life. Therefore, it is not <u>Real</u> God but the ego (perhaps gesturing conceptually toward "God") that is the source and fundamental "subject" of popular (or exoteric) "religion" (as well as higher mysticism). Real Transcendental Spiritual life begins only when the ego (with all of its mind, emotion, desire, and activity) is thoroughly understood and (thereby) transcended. For this reason, only the only-by-Me Revealed and Given "Radical" (and Perfectly ego-Transcending) Reality-Teaching of the seventh stage of life <u>directly</u> Serves the process of Most Perfect Real-God-Realization.* All other forms of doctrine (or instruction) serve the purposes of the first six stages of life—all of which are founded on the egoic presumption of "self-and-other".

It is the culture of conventional "religion" that promotes conventional ideas about "God". The principal conventional "God"-idea is that "God" is the "Creator" (or intentional Emanator) of the "worlds" and all beings. Such seems an obvious idea to the bodily ego, trapped in the mechanics of the perceptual mind and the material (or elemental) vision. The ego is identified with embodiment, and the idea of the "Creator-God" is developed to account for this fact, and to provide a conceptual basis (in the form of the idea of the ego as "God-made creature") for the appeal to "God" to Help the ego in this "world" and in the (yet unknown) after-death state.

The difficulty with the "Creator-God" conception is that it identifies "God" with ultimate "causation" and (thus) makes "God" inherently responsible for the subsequent "causation" of all "effects". And, if "God" is responsible for all "effects", then "God" is clearly a very powerful but also terrible Deity—since conditionally manifested existence tends to work both for and against all "creatures".

Therefore, in conventional "religious" thinking, the "Creator-God"-idea is commonly coupled with the idea of "God" as "Good" (and, thus, both opposite and opposed to "Evil"). If the "Creator-God" is conceived to be "Good" (or always working to positively "create", protect, nourish, rightly and pleasurably fulfill, and, ultimately, preserve all of conditional Nature and all "creatures"—insofar as they are rightly aligned to "God"), then the ego is free of the

---

* Avatar Adi Da uses the phrase "only-by-Me Revealed and Given" to indicate that His Reality-Way is not an effort or technique of the ego, but is rather His unique Gift of Divine Grace. "Most Perfect" is a technical term used by Avatar Adi Da to indicate the seventh stage of life.

emotional double-bind and the anger and despair that would seem to be justified if "God" is simply the responsible "Creator" of everything (good, bad, or in-between). Therefore, conventional "religious" theology is founded on both the idea of "God" as "Creator" and the idea of "God" as "Good" (or "Good Will").

However, if "God" is the All-Powerful "Creator" (except for Whose activities not anything has been made), then how did so much obviously negative (or evil) motion and "effect" come into existence? The usual answer is generally organized around one or another mythological story in which powerful creatures (or one powerful creature, such as "Satan", regarded to personify "Evil") entered (on the basis of free will) into a pattern of "sin" (or disobedience and conflict in relation to "God")—which resulted in separation from "God", and a descent (or fall) into gross (material) bondage, and so forth. Such mythologies are structured in terms of a hierarchical view of conditional Nature, with various planes descending from the "Heaven" of "God". "Religion" (thus) becomes a "method" of attempting to "return" to "God".

Exoteric "religion" (or the "God-religion" of the first three stages of life) is generally based on an appeal to belief, social morality, and magically effective prayer or worship. The "return" to "God" is basically conceived in terms of this "world"—and, therefore, exoteric (or terrestrial) "religion" is actually a process in which "God" returns to the ego and to this "world" (rather than vice versa), and it is believed that "God" will eventually reclaim humankind and the total "world" from the forces of "Evil". Nevertheless, exoteric "religion" is an "outer cult", intended for grosser egos and for mass consumption (or the culture of the first three stages of life). The most advanced form of conventional "God-religion" is the esoteric (or "inner") "cult"—which is a mystical society, open only to those chosen for initiation (and, thus, growth, or development, into the fourth and fifth stages of life).

Esoteric "God-religion" is a process of cosmic mysticism, or the "method" of "return" to "God" by ascending as mind (or disembodied "soul")—back through the route of the original fall into matter and "Evil"—until the "Heaven" (or "Eternal Abode") of "God" is reached again. This esoteric mystical process goes beyond the conventions of exoteric "religion" to develop the psycho-physical mechanics of mystical flight and "return" to "God" via the hierarchical structures of the nervous system (ascending from the plane of "Evil", or "Satan", or the "flesh", at the bodily base of the nervous system, to the plane of "God", or the plane of "Good", or the "Heavenly Abode", at or above the brain, via the "magic carpet" of the life-force in the nervous system).

Thus, the idea of the "Creator-God" leads to the idea that "God" is "Good" (or "Good Will"), which leads to the idea that "creatures" have free will, which then accounts for the appearance of "sin", suffering, "Evil", and loss of "God-consciousness". And conventional "God-religion" then becomes the means (through structures of belief, sacramental worship, mystical prayer, Yogic or shamanistic ascent, and so forth) for the re-exercise of "creaturely" free will in the direction of "God", "Good", the triumph over "Evil" and death in this "world", and the ascent from material form and consciousness to Spiritual, "Heavenly", or "Godly" form and consciousness.

All the popular "religious" traditions of humankind and all the mystical Spiritual traditions of humankind tend to be associated with this chain of conceptions (or the characteristic ideas of the first five stages of life). It is only in the sixth stage traditions that these ideas begin to give way to different conceptions. It is only in the sixth stage of life that the egoic basis of the first five stages of life is penetrated. And it is only in the only-by-Me Revealed and Given seventh stage of life that the ego is most perfectly transcended in the Divine Reality (Itself).

The Dogma of Atheism

The theological and general "religious" conceptions I have just Described have always been subject to criticism (or at least simple non-belief) on the part of those who are not persuaded by "religious" and theological arguments. Atheism (or the conception that no "Creator-God"—or any other Greater Reality—exists) has always opposed theism (or "God-religion"). Nevertheless, atheistic ideas are the product of the same fundamental egoic consciousness that otherwise produces theistic (or conventional "religious") ideas. Atheism is the product of the ego (or the phenomenal "self", grounded in elemental perception), and so also is theism. Atheism, like exoteric "God-religion", extends itself only into the domain of the first three stages of life—whereas esoteric "God-religion" provides a means for entering, mystically and Spiritually, into the developmental processes of the fourth stage of life and the fifth stage of life.

Atheism regularly proposes a "logic" of life that has its own dogmatic features. It does not propose a "God"-idea but, instead, founds itself on and in the perceptual and phenomenal mind alone. Atheism concedes only a universal and ultimately indifferent (or merely lawful) cosmic Nature (not a "God")—and, so, there is no need to create a "religious creation-myth" to account for suffering. (And atheistic thinkers thus generally confine themselves to constructing a cosmology, based on material observations alone, that merely accounts for the apparent workings of the conditionally manifested events of cosmic Nature.) Indeed, just as conventional "God-religion" (or conventional theism) arises to account for suffering, atheism arises on the basis of the unreserved acknowledgment of suffering. And, if there is no idea of "God", there is no idea of the human being as "creature" (or, in other words, the human being as the bearer of an immortal, or "God-like", "inner" part). Nor is there any need to interpret unfortunate or painful events as the "effects" of "Evil". Therefore, the atheistic "point of view" is characterized by the trend of mind called "realism", just as the conventional "religious" (or theistic) "point of view" is characterized by the trend of mind called "idealism"—but both atheism and theism arise on the basis of the "self"-contraction (or the ego of phenomenal "self"-consciousness), rather than on the basis of direct Intuition of the Real Self-Nature, Self-Condition, and Self-State That is Prior to separate "self" and its conventions of perception and thought.

The realistic (or atheistic) view is just as much the bearer of a myth (or a merely conceptual interpretation of the "world") as is the conventional "religious" (or theistic) view. Atheism (or conventional realism) is a state of mind which is based in the phenomenal "self" and which seeks the ultimate protection, nourishment, pleasure, and preservation of the phenomenal "self" (at least in this "world" and, if there should be an after-life, then also in any other "world"). Therefore, atheism (or conventional realism) is simply a philosophical alternative to theism (or conventional "God-religion"), based on the same principle and consciousness (which is the phenomenal ego), and seeking (by alternative means) to fulfill the conditionally manifested "self" and relieve it of its suffering.

Atheism (or conventional realism) is a state of mind that possesses individuals who are fixed in the first three stages of life. It is a form of "spiritual neurosis" (or ego-possession), as are all of the characteristic mind-states of the first six stages of life. Esoteric "God-religion" provides a basis for certain remarkable individuals to enter the fourth stage of life and the fifth stage of life, but the commonly (or exoterically) "religious" individual is, like the atheist, a relatively adolescent (if not childish, and even infantile) character, fixed in the ego-possessed states characteristic of the first three stages of life.

Atheism proposes a myth and a "method" for ego-fulfillment that is based on phenomenal realism, rather than "religious" idealism (or the culture of the conventional "God"-idea). Therefore, atheism is traditionally associated with the philosophy of materialism—just as theism is associated with "Creationism", and "Emanationism", and conventional (or mystical, or fourth and fifth stage) Spirituality. And the realistic (or atheistic) view tends to be the foundation for all kinds of political, social, and technological movements, since its orientation is toward the investigation and manipulation of material Nature.

Atheism is realism and materialism. It is about the acquisition of "knowledge" about conditional Nature and the exploitation of that "knowledge" to command (or gain power over) conditional Nature. And it is this scheme of "knowledge" and power (expressed as political and technological means of all kinds) that is the basis of the mythology and quasi-"religion" of atheism. The atheistic (or non-theistic) view of life is ego-based, organized relative to conditional Nature as an elemental (or grossly perceived) process, and committed to "knowledge" and power as the means of "salvation" (or material fulfillment of egoity).

In this "late-time" (or "dark" epoch), the materialistic, realistic, and non-theistic philosophy of ego-fulfillment is represented by the global culture of scientific, technological, and political materialism. The entire race of humankind is now being organized by the cultural movement of scientific materialism—which counters (and even seeks to suppress) the alternative cultures of exoteric "religion", esoteric mysticism, Transcendental Self-Realization, and Divine Enlightenment. Scientism (or the culture of realistic or materialistic "knowledge") and its two arms of power (technology and political order) are the primary forces in global culture of the present time. And humanity at large is (thus) tending to be reduced to the robotic acculturations of orderly egoism in the limited terms represented by humanity's functional development in the first three stages of life.

The Common Root-Error
of Both Theism and Atheism

Conventional and popular human culture has historically been limited to the conflicts and alternatives
represented by theism and atheism, or egoic idealism and egoic realism. And the large-scale ordering of
humankind has always tended to be dominated by the politics of materialistic "knowledge" and power. It is simply that,
in the "late-time" (or "dark" epoch), the materialistic culture
is approaching the status of a worldwide mass-culture in
which all individuals will be controlled by a powerful and
materialistically oriented system of political and technological restriction.

The usual (or most commonly remarked) criticism of
theism (or conventional "God-religion") is based on the evidence of suffering and material limitation. Therefore, the
common arguments against theism are generally those proposed by the "point of view" of atheism. Likewise, the common arguments against atheism are generally those proposed by theism (which are based on an egoic appeal to the
evidence of "religious" history, cultic revelation, mystical
psychology, and psychic "experience"). For this reason,
there may seem to be only two basic cultural alternatives:
atheism and theism.

Theism and conventional "God-religion" are, at base, an
expression of egoity in the first three stages of life—just as is
the case with atheism and conventional materialism. Therefore, whenever theism (or conventional "God-religion")
becomes the base for political and social order, it inevitably
becomes the base for "knowledge" and power in the material
"world". And exoterically theistic regimes have historically

been equally as aggressive in the manipulation and suppression of humanity as have atheistic regimes. Exoteric theism is, at its base, egoic and fitted to "worldly" concerns. Therefore, when it achieves "worldly" power, it simply adopts the same general materialistic means that are adopted by atheism. "Knowledge" and power are the common tools of egoity, not merely the tools of atheism. In its esoteric forms, theism (or conventional "God-religion") can, via the exercises and attainments of Saints and mystics, apply "knowledge" and power to purposes that extend beyond the first three stages of life. However, in the terms of the first three stages of life (or the common and practical social order), theism (or conventional "God-religion") is inclined to make the same demands for social consciousness—and to apply fundamentally the same kind of political and authoritarian "techniques" for achieving obedience and order—as atheism and scientism. And the more important esoteric matters of Spiritual Wisdom, mystical "knowledge", and the transformative power of Sainthood or Adeptship are as much in doubt and disrepute in the common "religious" circles of theism as they are in scientific and atheistic circles.

All of this is to indicate that conventional "God-religion" (or theism)—and even all "religious", "Spiritual", and "Transcendental" pursuits of the first six stages of life—share a "root"-error (or limitation) with atheism and "worldly" culture. That error (or limitation) is the ego itself, or the presumptions and the seeking that are most basic to the conception of an independent phenomenal "self" in a (less than hospitable) phenomenal "world". Thus, what is ultimately to be criticized in conventional "God-religion" (or theism) is the same limit that is to be criticized in atheism and materialism. It is the ego, the phenomenal "self"-base—from which people tend to derive their conceptions of "God", cosmic Nature, life, and destiny.

Understanding Life
As A Play of Opposites

It is only when the egoic "root" of one's functional, "worldly", and "religious" or "Spiritual" life is inspected, understood, and transcended that "self", and "world", and Real God are seen in Truth. Therefore, it is necessary to understand your own egoic activity. It is necessary to aspire to Wisdom, Truth, and Enlightenment. All occupations derived from the ego-base are (necessarily) limited to egoity, and all conceptions that feed such egoic occupations are (necessarily) bereft of a right view of "self", "world", and Real God (Which Is the Acausal Divine Reality and Truth).

When the mechanics of egoity are transcended in "self"-understanding, then it becomes obvious that life (or conditionally manifested phenomenal existence) is simply a "play" of opposites. Neither "Good" (or "creation" and preservation) nor "Evil" (or destruction) finally wins. Conditional Nature, in all its planes, is inherently a dynamic. The "play" of conditional Nature, in all its forms and beings and processes, is not merely (or exclusively and finally) seeking the apparent "Good" of "self"-preservation (or the preservation and fulfillment of any particular form, "world", or being), nor is it merely (or exclusively and finally) seeking the apparent "Evil" of "self"-destruction (or the dissolution of any particular form, "world", or being). Rather, the "play" in conditional Nature is always in the direction of perpetuating the dynamics of the "play" itself—and, therefore, polarity, opposition, struggle, alternation, death, and cyclic repetition tend to be perpetuated as the characteristics of phenomenal existence. Therefore, the "play" of conditional Nature is always alternating between the appearance of dominance by one or the other of its two basic extremes. And the sign of this is in the inherent struggle that involves every conditionally apparent form, being, and process. The struggle is this dynamic "play" of opposites, but the import of it is not the absolute triumph of either half. Things and beings and processes arise, they move, they are transformed, and they disappear. No conditionally apparent thing or being or process is ultimately preserved—nor, by contrast, is there any absolute destruction. Cosmic Nature is a transformer—not merely a "creator" or a "destroyer".

To the ego (or present temporary form of being), "self"-preservation may seem to be the inevitable motive of being. Therefore, a struggle develops to destroy or escape the dynamic of conditional Nature by dominating "Evil" (or death) with "Good" (or immortality). This ideal gets expressed in the generally exoteric and Occidental (or more materialistic) efforts to conquer conditional Nature via "worldly knowledge" and power. However, it also gets expressed in the generally esoteric and Oriental (or more mystical) efforts to escape the plane of conditional Nature by ascent from materiality (or the "Evil" of the flesh) to "Heaven" (the "Good God" above the realm of conditional Nature).

When the ego (or "self"-contraction) is understood and transcended, then conditional Nature is seen in the Light of Reality Itself. And, in that case, the egoic struggle in conditional Nature or against conditional Nature is also understood and transcended. Then life ceases to be founded on the need to defeat the dynamic of conditional Nature via conventional "knowledge", power, immortality, or mystical escape. The "world" is no longer conceived as a drama of warfare between "Good" and "Evil". The righteousness of the search for the "Good" as a means of "self"-preservation disappears along with the "self"-indulgent and "self"-destructive negativity of possession by "Evil". In place of this dilemma of opposites, an ego-transcending and "world"-transcending (or cosmic-Nature-transcending) equanimity appears. In that equanimity, there is an Inherent Self-Radiance That Transcends the egoic dualities of "Good" and "Evil" (or the conventional polarities of the separate "self" in conditional Nature). That Self-Radiance Is the Free Radiance of egoless Love. In That Free Radiance, energy and attention are inherently free of the ego-bond, or the "self"-contraction, or the "gravitational effect" of phenomenal "self"-awareness. Therefore, dynamic equanimity, or the free disposition of egoless Love (rather than the egoic disposition in the modes of "Good" or "Evil"), is the "window" through which Real (Acausal) God* may be "seen" (or intuited)—not in the conventional mode of "Creator", the "Good", the "Other", or the "Heavenly Place", but as the Real (or Reality Itself), the Self-Evidently Divine Self-Nature, Self-Condition, and Self-State of all-and-All.

When Truth and Reality Are Intrinsically Obvious

The ultimate moment in the "play" of conditional Nature is not the moment of egoic success (or the temporary achievement of the apparently positive, or "Good", "effect"). The ultimate moment is beyond contradiction (or the dynamics of polarized opposites). It is the moment of equanimity, the still point (or "eye") in the midst of the wheel of Nature's motions and all the motivations of the born "self". The Truth—and the Real Self-Nature, Self-Condition, and Self-State—of "self" and cosmic Nature is Revealed only in that equanimity, beyond all stress and bondage of energy and attention.

This disposition of equanimity (or free energy and attention) is basic to the sixth and seventh stages of life. In the sixth stage of life, the disposition of equanimity provides the functional base for the ultimate and final investigation of the ego and the dynamics of conditional Nature. However, it is

---

* Avatar Adi Da uses the term "Acausal" in this phrase specifically to counter the conventional concepts of "God" as the "Creator" of the universe.

only in the only-by-Me Revealed and Given seventh stage of life that Fundamental (and Intrinsically egoless) Equanimity Is Inherent and Constant, expressing Prior (and Permanent) Divine Self-Realization.

It is in the only-by-Me Revealed and Given seventh stage of life that Real (Acausal) God, Truth Itself, or Reality Itself Is Intrinsically Obvious, Prior to every trace of egoity, dilemma, and seeking. Therefore, it is in the only-by-Me Revealed and Given seventh stage of life that Real (Acausal) God is truly proclaimed—not in the conventional mode of "Creator" (or of "Good"), but As the Real (or Reality Itself).

Real (Acausal) God Is the Transcendental, Inherently Spiritual, and Self-Evidently Divine Truth, Reality, Identity, Self-Nature, Self-Condition, and Self-State of egoic "self" and conditional Nature. In the only-by-Me Revealed and Given seventh stage of life, That Is Tacitly Obvious—and there is not anything that must be escaped or embraced for the Love-Bliss-Fullness of Most Perfect Real-God-Realization to be Actualized. It Is Inherently So.

Therefore, the only-by-Me Revealed and Given Reality-Way of Adidam (or Adidam Ruchiradam*) is not any egoic means for attaining Real-God-Realization. Rather, the only-by-Me Revealed and Given Reality-Way of Adidam Is Real-God-Realization Itself—through ego-transcending "Locating" and "Knowing" of My Divine Avataric Transcendental Spiritual Grace, Beyond all the "methods" of the first six stages of life.

Real (Acausal) God—or the Transcendental, Inherently Spiritual, Intrinsically egoless, and Self-Evidently Divine Reality (Prior to conditional "self", conditional "world", and the ego-bound conventions of "religion" and non-"religion")—Is the One and Only Truth of Reality Itself, and the One and Only Way of Right Life and Perfect Realization.

---

* "Ruchiradam" is a word coined by Avatar Adi Da, deriving from Sanskrit "Ruchira" (meaning "bright", or "radiant"). The compound reference "Adidam Ruchiradam" communicates that Adidam is the Way of devotional response to Avatar Adi Da Samraj—Who Is recognized as the "Bright" Itself, and Who Gives the Realization of His own "Bright" Self-Condition.

TACIT CERTAINTY
OF REAL GOD

At the conclusion of Part One, Avatar Adi Da declares that the tacit (wordless and mindless) certainty of God is always available. In that certainty, it is self-evidently the case that God is not the "Cause" of everything, but (rather) the Reality and the Truth and the Source-Potential of everything.

I t is part of the ego-game to think of "God" as the "First Cause", or the "Cause" of everything. However, <u>Real</u> God is not the "Cause" of anything.

Real (Acausal) God <u>Is</u> That within Which everything is arising.

Real (Acausal) God <u>Is</u> That Power of egoless Mere Being Which <u>Is</u> Vast, Infinite, and Beyond comprehension—Tacitly, Self-Evidently So.

Real (Acausal) God <u>Is</u> Reality Itself—all-and-All-Including <u>and</u> all-and-All-Transcending.

When you exercise Reality-intelligence, the tacit certainty of Real God is directly and tacitly registered, completely obvious, and (altogether) Self-Evident. In that case, you simply regard all of this conditional arising in the disposition of your tacit certainty, which always "leans" you toward the Reality-Divine. There is much more than that "leaning" to Realize, but tacit certainty of the Self-Evidence of Reality Itself establishes you in the constantly "Godward" disposition. Therefore, you must never forget to exercise the moment to moment disposition in which the Reality-Divine Is Tacitly, Obviously So.

You forget to exercise the tacit certainty of Intrinsic Reality-intelligence whenever you identify with the "lower" (or merely superficial) body-mind-"self". However, when you keep Intrinsic Reality-intelligence constantly alive, and (thus and thereby) keep the heart alive moment to moment, there is always a tacit certainty of egoless Real God—Which Is the Perfect Power of Being, Reality Itself, the Self-Evidently Divine Self-Nature, Self-Condition, and Self-State of all-and-All.

All kinds of ideas are prevalent in the various common institutions of "religion", and those ideas seem to be about "God". However, in actuality, those ideas are about human-kind, and about maintaining order among humankind—the order associated with civilized living, social life, political authority, the structuring of society. Thus, the concern of conventional "religious" institutions and processes is not Real-God-Realization but social, political, and cultural order.

My Divinely Avatarically Self-Revealed Reality-Teachings are not, in Their fundamentals, about social, political, and cultural order. My Divinely Avatarically Self-Revealed Reality-Teachings Are Direct Self-Revelations of Real-God-Realization. Therefore, My Divinely Avatarically Self-Revealed Reality-Teachings Are a Call for people to enter into the Real-God-Realizing Process. That is another matter altogether than the maintaining of social, political, and cultural order (either principally or for its own sake). Thus and so, the esoteric domain of the Real-God-Realizing Process transcends conventional "religion" of the common institutionalized kind.

Ideas such as "God the Creator", or "the God of history", or "the God Who does everything" are institutional ideas associated with conventional (and socially-oriented) "religion", not Communications from the "Disposition" of Real-God-Realization. Even though conventional ideas about "God" are associated with the "God"-label, such ideas are, in fact, ordinary human ideas.

The idea of the "Creator-God" suggests that "God" is responsible for everything that everybody does and everything that is happening. <u>Real</u> (Acausal) God Is the egoless Being-Force <u>within</u> Which all of this is arising. Therefore, you cannot hold Real (Acausal) God accountable for what <u>you</u> are doing, or for how "things" are happening, or (indeed) for all your trouble here.

Real (Acausal) God <u>Is</u> the Immense Resource, or the Source-Potential, for everything. Therefore, everything arises in and <u>As</u> Real (Acausal) God—but no "thing" or "event" is "caused" by Real (Acausal) God.

You yourself are making the "events" of your life, and always according to your own conclusions—and you yourself are fastening yourself to the limitations you choose. Real (Acausal) God is not responsible for any or all of that. Real (Acausal) God <u>Is</u> the Reality-Way Beyond all of that.

Real (Acausal) God <u>Is</u> That Which you must Intrinsically (or Always Priorly) Self-Realize in order to <u>Be</u> Intrinsically and Perfectly egolessly Liberated from all your apparent limitations.

Real (Acausal) God <u>Is</u> That Force of Being, That Immense Reality-Intelligence, That Incomprehensible Intelligence and egoless Perfect Force That Is the "Being-Reason" Why anything can be at all.

Therefore, Real (Acausal) God <u>Is</u> the Intrinsically Self-Evident Reality-Resort of all-and-All—and the Ultimate Potential and Possibility of all-and-All.

Such <u>Is</u> the True Nature of Real (Acausal) God.

Devotion to the Realizer is the ancient Way of true Spiritual life.

I have characterized devotion to the Realizer as the "ancient Walk-About Way"—indicating that devotion to the Realizer has been the Way since before history was written.

Devotion to the Realizer is the "pre-civilization Way", which existed before any recorded history, during a time when human beings were, essentially, merely wandering all over the Earth.

Devotion to the Realizer has always been the fundamental Means of human Spirituality, whatever other teachings have been given in the circumstance of devotion to any Realizer.

AVATAR ADI DA SAMRAJ

PART TWO

How Truth
and Reality
Are Revealed

ADEPT-REALIZERS ARE THE ROOT
OF ALL ESOTERIC TRADITIONS

Part Two begins with Avatar Adi Da's exposition of the great traditional knowledge that those who have actually <u>Realized</u> Truth and Reality (the Adept-Realizers) are at the core of all genuine Spiritual Revelations. It is the Adept-Realizers who make the <u>Realization</u> of Truth and Reality possible for others.

1.

The primary force and "root" of all the esoteric traditions of humankind are the Adept-Realizers, those who actually Realize (to one or another degree) the Spiritual and Transcendental Nature of Reality. Adept-Realizers (in their various degrees and kinds of Realization) appear in all times and places, and they become associated with the complex social and cultural structures existing in their immediate environment. Throughout their lifetimes, both before and after their Realization, such Adepts move into the existing culture and associate with its influences. Thus, while the teaching of any Adept is, of course, an expression of his or her actual Realization, the Adept's words also reflect and comment upon all kinds of cultural complexities and ideals. Where Adept-Realizers appear, they transform the existing culture, eliminating some aspects of traditional "religious" and Spiritual life and emphasizing others. The Spiritually Realized Adept is a motion in the midst of the stream of conventions.

The tradition of Truth, the tradition of Spiritual and Transcendental Realization, is the tradition of the Adept-Realizers. Apart from the Adepts, there is no tradition of Truth.

2.

In all "religious" and Spiritual traditions, a great deal is made of some key individual. There is no great Spiritual tradition that is without a person at the center of the process. How that person is interpreted through the cultural and intellectual lore of each tradition varies, but such an individual always exists. In other words, the Truth is not separable from a special human function that is perceived in the form of the Adept-Realizer, or Spiritual Master (or Guru).

3.

The Adept-Realizer, or Spiritual Master, has many functions—to exemplify the Way, to argue the Way, to Bless devotees, and (thus) to interfere with the usual attitude and disposition of devotees, and to Transmit Spiritual Influence tangibly to devotees so that they will then, having understood themselves, be capable of Spiritual growth. The function of the Spiritually Realized Adept, therefore, does not come to an end with the arising of any particular result. The Adept-Realizer (or Guru) is the continuous and unending resource and resort of his or her devotees.

4.

One who Functions as Adept Spiritual Master (or as a Realizer-Guru) exercises the Guru-Function only in relation to those who are his or her devotees. If the Adept addresses public society at all, he or she may also (in the public setting) assume the role of prophet—which is, essentially, an aggravation, a criticism, an undermining of the usual life.

5.

Adept-Realizers of one or another degree of Spiritual development spontaneously Transmit That Which they have Realized. That Which they have Realized Transmits Itself— subtly as well as in the gross physical dimension—by what they do, by what they are, by what they feel. Thus, accordingly, Adept-Realizers Transmit their degree of Realization. Such Transmission is inevitable, and Such Transmission is an absolute Law. This is why, traditionally, it is said that the best thing anyone can do, among all the things everyone must do—and you must do many things—the best among them, the chief among them, is to spend time in the Company of an Adept-Realizer, or Spiritual Master.

Everything transmits. The stones transmit, the sky transmits, the TV transmits. Since everything and everyone transmits states of existence—since life, or existence itself, is participation in transmissions of all kinds—the best thing you can do is to associate with the greatest possible Transmission. Since everything is transmission, spend time in the Company of the One Who spontaneously Transmits That Which Is Inherently Perfect and Ultimate.

This is the Great Rule, the Great Law, the Ultimate Principle of the Great Tradition* of humankind.

6.

Devotional allegiance to the Adept-Realizer, or Spiritual Master, is the greatest function of existence and the single advantage not only of human beings but of all beings. The devotional relationship to the Spiritual Master is participation in a unique function that appears in the realm of cosmic (or conditional) Nature.

---

* "Great Tradition" is Avatar Adi Da's term for the total inheritance of human, cultural, religious, magical, mystical, Spiritual, and Transcendental paths, philosophies, and testimonies, from all the eras and cultures of humankind.

Only the ego will deny the Spiritual Master. The ego wants to "do it" himself or herself. Do <u>what</u> exactly? <u>Be</u> himself or herself—separately and untouched. Since you become what you meditate on,* you should meditate on, or give feeling-attention to, the Absolute—which, in the bodily (human) form of the Spiritual Master, is your greatest advantage.

7.

No thought or figure or any perception arising in the mind is, in and of itself, Real (Acausal) God. No thing, no body, no moment or place is, in and of itself, Real (Acausal) God. Rather, every moment, place, thing, body, or state of mind <u>inheres</u> in the Divine Reality and Truth That <u>Is</u> Real (Acausal) God. Thus, all conditions become Reminders that draw the devotee into Divine Communion.

The Spiritual Master is a Transparent Reminder of the Divine Reality, a Guide to the ecstatic Realization of the One Reality in Which all conditions arise and change and pass away. The Spiritual Master is not to be made into the merely "objectified" idol of a cult, as if the Divine Being were exclusively contained in the "objective" person and "subjective" beliefs of a particular sect. Rather, right relationship to the Spiritual Master takes the form of free devotional response to the Spiritual Master's Radiant State.

---

* Avatar Adi Da indicates that this traditional esoteric law—that "you become what you meditate on"—is an essential means of understanding how the devotional relationship to the Adept-Realizer works. The persistent practice of giving one's attention to (or "meditating on") the Adept-Realizer awakens direct Communion with the Realizer's State.

THE GREAT ESOTERIC
TRADITION OF DEVOTION
TO THE ADEPT-REALIZER

In this summary essay, Avatar Adi Da expounds further on the import of transformative relationship with the Adept-Realizer—and elaborates the fundamental Spiritual principles that underlie this unique relationship. He also addresses ways in which the characteristics of modern, secularized culture suppress and effectively deny this crucial means by which humankind has always been served.

The Great Principle
of Spiritual Practice

Spiritually Realized Adepts (or Transmission-Masters, or True Gurus) are the principal Sources, Resources, and Means of the esoteric (or Spiritual) Way. This fact is not (and never has been) a matter of controversy among real Spiritual practitioners.

The entire Spiritual Way is a process based on the understanding (and the transcending) of attention, or the understanding (and the transcending) of the inevitable and specific results of egoic attachment to, or egoic reaction to, or egoic "self"-identification with every kind of conditional "object", other, or state. This Spiritual understanding (or real "self"-understanding) is expressed in a simple traditional formula (and prescription for practice): You become (or duplicate the qualities of) whatever you meditate on (or whatever you identify with via the "surrender" that is attention itself). Since the most ancient days, this understanding has informed and inspired the practice of real practitioners of the Spiritual Way. Likewise (since the most ancient days), and on the basis of this very understanding, Spiritual practitioners have affirmed that the Great Principle of Spiritual practice is devotional Communion with the Realized Adept, or the practice of life as "self"-surrender to the bodily Person, the Transmitted Spiritual Presence, and the Realized State of a Spiritually Realized Adept (or True Guru) of whatever degree or stage.

The Great Function of The Adept As Guru

The traditional term "Guru" (spelled with a capital "G") means "One Who Reveals the Light and thereby Liberates beings from Darkness". This term is also commonly (or popularly) interpreted in a general (or everyday) sense (and spelled with a small "g") to mean "teacher" (or anyone who teaches anything at all to another). Thus, Adepts have certainly (and rightly) been valued simply (or in the general sense) as (small "g") "gurus" (that is, simply because they can instruct others about many things, including the Spiritual Way). However, the function of instruction (about anything at all) can be performed by anyone who is properly informed (or even by a book that is properly informed)—and, indeed, even the specific function of Spiritual Instruction is secondary to the Great Function of the Adept (As Guru, with a capital "G").

Adepts inevitably (or, at least, in the majority of cases) Instruct (or Teach) others, but the function of Instruction (about the Spiritual Way) is then passed on through good books (containing the authentic Word of Teaching), and through informed others (who are, hopefully, true practitioners), and so forth. The Great Function of the Adept-Guru is, however, specific only to Adepts themselves, and this is the Guru-Function (and the Guru-Principle) supremely valued by Spiritual practitioners since the most ancient days.

The Secret
of Realization

The specific Guru-Function is associated with the Great Principle of devotional Communion with the Adept-Guru (and with the unique Spiritual understanding of attention). Therefore, since the most ancient days, all truly established (or real) Spiritual practitioners have understood that devotional Communion with the Adept-Guru is, Itself, the Great Means for Realizing Real (Acausal) God, or Truth Itself, or Reality Itself. That is to say, the Great Means (or Secret) of Realization in the Spiritual Way is to live in, or to spend significant time in, or otherwise (and constantly) to give attention to the Company, Form, Presence, and State* of an Adept who is (truly) Realized in one or another of the esoteric stages of life.

The Essence of the practice of devotional Communion with the Adept-Guru is to focus attention on (and thereby to, in due course, become Identified with, or Realize Indivisible Oneness with) the Realized Condition of a True Adept-Guru (especially One Who Is presently and constantly In Samadhi† or in the actual State of True Realization, however, and by whatever term of reference, Realization is described in any particular tradition or school). Therefore, the practice of devotional Communion with the Adept-Guru is the practice of ego-transcending Communion (and, Ultimately, Indivisible Oneness) with the Adept's own Condition,

---

* Here Avatar Adi Da Samraj is using "Form" to mean the physical body, "Presence" to mean the Spiritual Radiance, and "State" to mean the Realized Condition of an Adept-Realizer.

† The Sanskrit word "Samadhi" traditionally denotes various exalted states that appear in the context of esoteric meditation and Realization.

Which Is (according to the degree or stage of the Adept's characteristic Realization) Samadhi Itself, or the Adept's characteristic (and Freely, Spontaneously, and Universally Transmitted) Realization (Itself).

The Principle of Independent self-Effort Versus The Principle of Supreme Attraction

B ased on the understanding of attention (or the observation that Consciousness Itself, in the context of the body-mind-"self", tends to identify with, or becomes fixed in association with, whatever attention observes, and especially with whatever attention surrenders to most fully), the Spiritual Motive is essentially the Motive to transcend the limiting capability of attention (or of all conditional "objects", others, and states). Therefore, the traditional Spiritual process (as a conventional "technique", begun in the context of the fourth stage of life) is an effort (or struggle) to set attention (and, thus, Consciousness Itself) Free by progressively relinquishing attachment and reaction to conditional "objects", others, and states (and, Ultimately, this process requires the Most Perfect transcending of egoity, or "self"-contraction itself, or all the egoic limitations associated with each and all of the first six stages of life).

This conventional effort (or struggle) is profound and difficult, and it tends to progress slowly. Therefore, some few adopt the path of extraordinary "self"-effort (or a most intense struggle of relinquishment), which is asceticism (or the "method" of absolute independence). However, the Adepts themselves have, since the most ancient days, offered an alternative to mere (and, at best, slowly progressing) "self"-effort. Indeed, the Adept-Gurus offer a Unique Principle of practice (as an alternative to the conventional principle of mere and independent "self"-effort and relinquishment). That Unique Principle is the Principle of Supreme Attraction.

Truly, the bondage of attention to conditional "objects", others, and states must be really transcended in the Spiritual Way, but mere "self"-effort (or struggle with the separate, and separative, "self") is a principle that originates in (and constantly reinforces) the separate (and separative) "self" (or "self"-contraction, or egoity itself). Therefore, the process of the real transcending of bondage to conditions is made direct (and truly ego-transcending) if the principle of independent "self"-effort (or egoic struggle) is (at least progressively) replaced by the responsive (or cooperative) Principle of Supreme Attraction (Which Is, in Its Fullness, responsive devotional and Spiritual Identification with the Free Person, Presence, and State of One Who Is Already Realized, or In Samadhi).

The Ancient Essence of The Spiritual Way

On the basis of the simple understanding of attention—expressed in the formula: You become (or Realize) What (or Who) you meditate on—the ancient Essence of the Spiritual Way is to meditate on (and otherwise to grant feeling-attention to) the Adept-Guru, and (thereby) to be Attracted (or Grown) beyond the "self"-contraction (or egoity, or all the "self"-limiting tendencies of attention, or all "self"-limiting and "self"-binding association with conditional "objects", others, and states). Through sympathetic (or responsive) Spiritual Identification with the Spiritually Self-Transmitted State of a Realizer, the devotee is Spiritually Infused and (potentially) Awakened by the Inherently Attractive Power of That State Itself. Even the simplest beginner in practice may be directly Inspired—and, thus, moved toward greater practice, true devotion, and eventual Spiritual Awakening—by sympathetic response to the Free Sign, and the Great Demonstration, of a True Realizer. And, by the

Great Spiritual Means That Is true devotional Communion with a True Realizer (coupled with a variety of disciplines and practices, which should be associated with real "self"-understanding), the fully prepared devotee of a True Realizer may Freely (or with relative effortlessness) relinquish (or Grow Beyond) the limits of attention relative to each of the progressive stages of life that, in due course, follow upon that devotion.

Of course, actual Spiritual Identification with the Realized Spiritual Condition of an Adept is limited by the stage of life of the devotee, the effective depth of the "self"-understanding and the ego-transcending devotional response of the devotee, and the stage of life and Realization of the Adept. And some traditions may (unfortunately) tend to replace (or, at least, to combine) the essential and great practice of devotional Communion with the Adept-Guru with concepts and norms associated with the parent-child relationship, or the relationship between a king and a frightened subject, or even the relationship between a slave-master and a slave. However, this Great Principle (or Means) of devotional Communion with the Adept-Guru (rightly understood and truly practiced) is the ancient Essence (or Great Secret) of the Spiritual Way—and True Adept-Gurus have, therefore, since the most ancient days, been the acknowledged principal Sources and Resources (as well as the principal Means) of right "religious" practice (or effective "religious" Wisdom) and the esoteric tradition of Spiritual Realization.

The Mood of
Adolescent Rebellion Against Authority

Particularly in more modern days, since Spirituality (and everything else) has become a subject of mass communication and popularization, the Spiritual Way Itself has become increasingly subject to conventional interpretation and popular controversy. In the broad social (or survival) context of the first three stages of life, "self"-fulfillment (or the consolation of the ego) is the common ideal (tempered only by local, popular, and conventional political, social, and "religious" ideals, or demands). Therefore, the common mood is one of adolescent anti-authority and anti-hierarchy (stemming from the "Oedipal"* anti-"parent" disposition), and the common search is for a kind of ever-youthful (and "Narcissistic") ego-omnipotence and ego-omniscience.

The popular egalitarian (or ego-based, and merely, and competitively, individualistic) "culture" (or, really, anticulture) of the first three stages of life is characterized by the politics of adolescent rebellion against "authority" (or the perceived "parent", in any form). Indeed, a society (or any loose collective) of mere individuals does not feel the need for, and cannot (by tendency alone) even much tolerate, a true culture—because a true culture must, necessarily, be characterized (in its best, and even general, demonstrations, and, certainly, in its aspirations) by mutual tolerance, cooperation, peace, and profundity. Therefore, societies based on competitive individualism, and egoic "self"-fulfillment, and mere gross-mindedness (or superficial-mindedness) actually tend to suppress and even destroy right culture (and all until-then-existing right cultures, and right cultural

---

* In modern psychology, the "Oedipus complex" is named after the legendary Greek Oedipus, who was fated to unknowingly kill his father and marry his mother. Avatar Adi Da Teaches that the primary dynamics of emotional-sexual desiring, rejection, envy, betrayal, "self"-pleasuring, resentment, and other primal emotions and impulses are (as first systematically suggested by Sigmund Freud) patterned upon unconscious reactions formed early in life, in relation to one's mother and father.

adaptations). And right cultures (and right cultural adaptations) are produced (and needed) only when individuals
rightly and truly participate in a collective, and, thus and
thereby, live in accordance with the life-principle of transcending egoity and the Great Principle of Inherent Oneness
(or Prior Unity).

In the popular egalitarian (or ego-based, and merely,
and competitively, individualistic) "culture" (or, really, anticulture) of the first three stages of life, the Guru and the
developmental culture of the Spiritual Way are (with even all
of "authority" and of true, or ego-transcending, culture)
more or less taboo, because every individual limited (or
egoically defined) by the motives of the first three stages of
life is at war with personal vulnerability and need (or the
feeling of egoic insufficiency). However, the real Spiritual
process does not even begin until the egoic "point of view"
of the first three stages of life is understood (or otherwise
ceases to be the limit of aspiration and awareness) and the
ego-surrendering and ego-transcending Motive of the fourth
stage of life begins to move and change the body-mind
(from the heart).

Those who are truly involved in the ego-surrendering
and ego-transcending process of the esoteric stages of life
are (fundamentally) no longer at war with their own Help—
and, thus, they are no longer struggling toward the ultimate
victory of the ego. Therefore, it is only in the non-Spiritual
(or even anti-Spiritual) "cultural" domain of the first three
stages of life (or the conventional survival-culture, bereft
of the Motive of truly developmental and Spiritual culture)
that the Guru is, in principle, taboo. And, because that taboo
is "rooted" in adolescent reactivity and egoic willfulness (or
the yet unresolved emotional, and psychological, and even
emotional-sexual rebellion against childish and emotionally
and sexually ego-suppressing dependence on parent-like
individuals and influences), "anti-Guruism", and even

"anti-cultism"—which (characteristically, and without discrimination) denigrate, and defame, and mock, or otherwise belittle, <u>all</u> "authorities", and (also) even all the seed-groups of newly emerging cultural movements (whether or not they have positive merit)—are forms (or expressions) of what Sigmund Freud described as an "Oedipal" problem.

Cultism, Intellectualism, and "Anti-Guruism"

In the common "world" of humankind, it is yet true that most individuals tend (by a combination of mechanical psycho-physical tendencies and a mass of conventional political, social, and cultural pressures) to be confined to the general "point of view" associated, developmentally, with the unfinished (or yet to be understood) "business" of the first three stages of life. Thus, in the common "world" of humankind, even "religion" is (characteristically) reduced to what is intended to serve the "creaturely" (or "worldly"), and rather aggressively <u>exoteric</u>, "point of view" and purposes of egoity in the context of the first three stages of life. And even if an interest in the <u>esoteric</u> possibilities (beyond the first three stages of life) develops in the case of any such (yet rather "worldly") character, that interest tends to be pursued in a manner that dramatizes and reinforces the "point of view" (and the exoteric, and either childishly or adolescently egoic, inclinations) characteristic of the first three stages of life.

Until there is the development of significantly effective "self"-understanding relative to the developmental problems (or yet unfinished "business") associated with the first three stages of life, any one who aspires to develop a truly esoteric practice (necessarily beginning in the context of the fourth stage of life) will, characteristically, tend to relate to such possible esoteric practice in either a childish or an adolescent manner. Thus, any one whose developmental disposition is yet relatively childish (or tending, in general, to seek egoic security via the dramatization of the role of emotionalistic dependency) will tend to relate to esoteric possibilities via emotionalistic (or, otherwise, merely enthusiastic) attachments, while otherwise (in general) tending to be weak in both the responsible exercise of discriminating intelligence and the likewise responsible exercise of functional, practical, relational, and cultural* "self"-discipline. (Indeed, such childish religiosity, characterized by dependent emotionalism, or mere enthusiastic attachment, bereft of discrimination and real "self"-discipline, is what may rightly, without bad intentions, be described and criticized as "cultism".) And any one whose developmental disposition is yet relatively adolescent (or tending, in general, to seek egoic security via the dramatization of the role of reactive independence) will tend to relate to esoteric possibilities via generally "heady" (or willful, rather mental, or even intellectual, or bookish, but not, altogether, truly intelligent) efforts, accompanied either (or even alternately) by a general lack of "self"-discipline (and a general lack of non-reactive emotional responsiveness) or by an exaggerated (abstractly enforced, and more or less life-suppressing and emotion-suppressing) attachment to "self"-discipline. Such adolescent, or "heady", religiosity merely continues the dramatization of the characteristic adolescent search for independence, or the reactive pursuit of escape from every kind of dependency, and (altogether) the reactive pursuit of egoic "self"-sufficiency. And such adolescent seeking is inherently and reactively disinclined toward any kind of "self"-surrender. Therefore, the rather adolescent seeker tends to want to be his or her own "guru" in all matters. And, characteristically, the rather adolescent seeker will resist, and would even prefer to avoid, a

---

* Avatar Adi Da uses the phrase "functional, practical, relational, and cultural" to describe a range of disciplines relative to right action and responsibility that covers all basic areas of human life, such as diet, health, exercise, sexuality, work, service, cooperative living, meditation, and worship.

truly intelligent, rightly "self"-disciplined, and (altogether) devotionally "self"-surrendered relationship to a True Guru.

Because of their developmental tendencies toward either childish or adolescent ego-dramatizations, those who are yet bound to the "point of view" (or the unfinished "business") of the first three stages of life are, developmentally (or in their characteristic disposition, which is not yet relieved by sufficient "self"-understanding), also (regardless of their presumed "interest") not yet truly ready to enter into the esoteric process (beyond the first three stages of life). And, for the same developmental reasons, the principal and most characteristic impediments toward true participation in the esoteric process are "cultism" (or mere emotionalistic dependency, bereft of discrimination and "self"-discipline), "intellectualism" (or merely mental, or even bookish, preoccupation, disinclined to fully participatory, or directly "experiential", involvement in the esoteric process), and "anti-Guruism" (or reactive attachment to a state of egoic independence, immune to the necessity for devotional "self"-surrender and the Grace of Great Help).

The Heart's Great Impulse
To Grow Beyond

It is not the specific (and Great) Function of the Adept to fulfill a popular Spiritual (or, otherwise, non-Spiritual) role in common (or egoic and early-stage) society, but to Serve as Teacher, Guide, Spiritual Transmitter, or Free Awakener in relation to those who are already (and rightly) moved (and progressively prepared) to fulfill the ego-transcending obligations of the Great and (soon) Spiritual Way Itself (in the potential developmental context that is beyond the first three stages of life). The only proper relationship to such a Realized Adept (or True Guru) is, therefore, one of real and right and ego-surrendering and ego-transcending practice, and that practice must, from the beginning, be practically Inspired (and, soon, Spiritually Inspired) by ego-transcending devotion—not childish egoity (characterized by "cultic" dependency), and not adolescent egoity (characterized by willful or, otherwise, ambivalent independence).

Of course, individuals in the earlier (or first three) stages of life who are not yet actively oriented (or, otherwise, rightly adapted) to ego-surrendering and ego-transcending practice may be Served by Adept-Gurus, but (apart from special instances where an Adept must Work directly with such individuals, in order to establish a new cultural gathering of devotees, or in order to establish a new Revelation of the Spiritual Way) those not yet actively oriented (or actively committed), or (otherwise) rightly adapted, to truly ego-surrendering and really ego-transcending practice are generally (except perhaps for occasional glimpses of the Adept in his or her Free Demonstration) Served (or prepared for ego-surrendering, ego-transcending, and, soon, Spiritual practice) only through the written (or otherwise recorded) Teachings of an Adept, and through the public institutional work (and the "outer temple", or beginner-serving, institutional work) of the practicing devotees of an Adept.

The Realized Adept (or any True Guru) is, primarily, an esoteric Figure, whose unique Function Serves within the context of the esoteric stages of life. The esoteric stages of life are themselves open only to those who are ready, willing, and able to make the Real-God-Realizing (or Truth-Realizing, or Reality-Realizing) sacrifice of separate and separative "self" that is necessary in the context of the esoteric stages of life. Therefore, the necessity (and the True Nature and Great Function) of a Realized Adept (or True Guru) is obvious (and of supreme value) only to those who are ready, willing, and able to embrace the ego-transcending process of the esoteric stages of life.

Except for the possible moments in which the Acausal Divine Person (or the Ultimate Reality and Truth) may (for some few) Serve (temporarily, and, to whatever degree, significantly, and, in any case, never to the Most Ultimate, or Most Perfect, degree) in (or via) a non-physical (and/or perhaps even non-human) Revelation-Form, the devotional relationship to the Realized Adept is an absolute (and never obsolete) necessity for any and every human being who would practice (and Realize) within the esoteric stages of life. Therefore, the necessity (and the True Nature and Great Function) of a Realized Adept (or True Guru) is inherently (and gratefully) obvious to any one and every one who is truly ready, willing, and able to embrace the esoteric process of Real-God-Realization (or Reality-Realization).

Any one and every one who doubts and quibbles about the necessity (and the True Nature and Great Function) of a True Adept-Guru is, simply, not yet ready, willing, and able to enter the (necessarily, ego-surrendering) process of the esoteric stages of life. And no mere verbal (or otherwise exoteric) argument is sufficient to convince such doubters of the necessity (and the True Nature and Great Function) of a True Adept-Guru—just as no mere verbal (or otherwise exoteric) argument is sufficient to make them ready, willing, and able to truly embrace the ego-surrendering process of the esoteric stages of life.

Those who doubt the Guru-Principle, and the unique value and ultimate necessity of the Adept-Guru, are those for whom the Great and (soon) Spiritual Way Itself is yet in doubt. Therefore, such matters remain "controversial"—and access to the Spiritual Way and the Adept-Company continues to be effectively denied to ordinary people by the popular taboos and the psychological limitations of the first three stages of life—until the Real-God-Realizing Motive Awakens the heart's Great Impulse to Grow Beyond.

BEYOND THE CULTIC TENDENCY
IN RELIGION AND SPIRITUALITY,
AND IN SECULAR SOCIETY

This essay presents Avatar Adi Da's essential criticism of the tendency to create "cults" around Adept-Realizers and His call to observe, understand, and transcend the cultic tendency as it operates in every area of human life.

In My Reality-Teaching, I Speak critically of the conventional (or childish, and, otherwise, adolescent) orientation of "Guru-cultism". Such cultism is a tendency that has <u>always</u> been present in the "religious" and Spiritual traditions of humankind. Anciently, and in the present time, both true Spiritual Masters and ordinary Wisdom-Teachers have been "cultified", and (thereby) made the merely fascinating "Object" of a self-contained popular movement that worships the Spiritual Master as a Parent-like Savior, while embracing very little of the significant Wisdom-Teaching of the Spiritual Master.

The error of conventional cultism is precisely this childish, and (otherwise) adolescent, and (altogether) <u>ego-based</u> orientation to fascination with Spiritual Masters, Wisdom-Teachers, "God"-Ideas, myths, sacred lore, inherited beliefs, traditional propaganda, and psycho-physical (or merely body-mind-based) mysticism. And the cultic tendency in "religion" and Spirituality is the essence of what is wrong with conventional "religion" and Spirituality.

The "problem" is <u>not</u> that there <u>Is</u> no Real God, or that there are no true Wisdom-Teachings, or that there are no

98

true Spiritual Masters, or that there should be no devotion to any true Spiritual Masters. The "problem" with conventional "religion" and Spirituality is the same as the "problem" of all ordinary life. The "problem" is the childish, and (otherwise) rather adolescent, egoism that is the basis of all forms of ordinary existence.

Yet un-Enlightened (or, otherwise, not yet Most Perfectly Enlightened) people are ego-possessed. Therefore, egoity is the "disease" that all the true Spiritual Masters come here to cure. Unfortunately, those who are merely fascinated by Spiritual Masters are, typically, those who make (or, at least, transform) the institutions of the Way of their Spiritual Masters. And true practitioners of any "religious" or Spiritual Way are very hard to find, or develop. Therefore, "religious" and Spiritual institutions tend to develop along lines that serve, accommodate, and represent the common egoity— and this is why the esoteric true Teachings of true Spiritual Masters tend to be bypassed, and even suppressed, in the drive to develop the exoteric cult of any particular Spiritual Master.

The relationship to Me that is Described (by Me) in My Reality-Teaching is not an exoteric cultic matter. It is a profound esoteric discipline, necessarily associated with real and serious and mature (ego-surrendering, ego-forgetting, ego-transcending, and Divine-Guru-Oriented) practice of the "Radical" Way (or "Root"-Process) of Realizing Real (Acausal) God (Which Is Reality Itself and Truth Itself). Therefore, I am critical of the ego-based (or "self"-saving, and "self-guruing") practices of childish, and (otherwise) adolescent, and (altogether) merely exoteric cultism.

The common "religious" or Spiritual cult is based on the tendency to resist the disciplines of real (and really ego-transcending) practice, and to opt for mere fascination with extraordinary (or even imaginary) phenomena (which are, invariably, not understood in Truth and in Reality). Apart from the often petty demand for the observation of conventional rules (generally, relative to social morality, or merely social "religion"), the cult of "religious" and Spiritual fascination tends to become righteously associated with no practice—that is, with the even "official" expectation that there be no real (or truly right, and full) practice of "religious" and Spiritual disciplines (especially of Spiritual and meditative disciplines of an esoteric kind). Likewise, the cult of "religious" and Spiritual fascination tends to be equally righteous about maintaining fascinated faith (or indiscriminate, and even aggressive, belief) in the merely Parent-like "Divine" Status of one or another historical individual, "God"-idea, "religious" or Spiritual doctrine, inherited tradition, or force of cosmic Nature. "Religious" and Spiritual cultism is, thus, a kind of infantile collective madness. (And such madness is equally shared by secular cultists, in every area of popular culture—including politics, the sciences, the arts, the communications media, and even all the agencies and institutions of conventional "officialdom" relative to human "knowledge", belief, and behavior.) "Religious" and Spiritual cults (and, likewise, all secular cults) breed "pharisaism" (or the petty righteousness of conventional thinking). "Religious" and Spiritual cults breed "substitution" myths (or the belief that the personal transcending of egoity is, both generally and ultimately, impossible—but also unnecessary, because of what "God", or some "Master", or even some "priest" has already done). Indeed, "religious" and Spiritual cults (and, likewise, all secular cults) breed even every kind of intolerance, and the chronic aggressive search for exclusive social dominance and secular power. "Religious" and Spiritual cults are, characteristically, populated by those who are, generally, neither inclined toward nor prepared for the real right practice of "religious" and Spiritual discipline, but who are (and always seek to be) glamorized and consoled by mere association with the "holy" things and beliefs of the cult itself.

This error of "religious" and Spiritual cultism, and of ego-based culture in general, must be examined very seriously—such that the error is truly rooted out, from within the cult and the culture itself (and not merely, and with equally cultic cultural righteousness, criticized from without). Cultism of every kind (both sacred and secular) must be understood to be a kind of ritualized infantilism—bound to egocentric behavior, and to the embrace of "insiders" only, and to intolerance relative to all "outsiders". The cultic tendency, both sacred and secular, brings about (and has always brought about) great social, cultural, and political trouble—as has been seen, in this "late-time" (or "dark" epoch), in the development of worldwide conflicts based on the exclusive (or collectively egocentric) orientation of the many grossly competitive "religious" traditions, political idealisms, and national identities.

All cults, whether sacred or secular, thrive on indulgence in the psychology (and the emotional rituals) of hope, rather than on actual demonstration of really ego-transcending action. Therefore, when all egos meet, they strive and compete for the ultimate fulfillment of searches and desires, rather than cooperate with Truth Itself, Reality Itself, or Real (Acausal) God, and in a culturally valued and rewarded mood of fearless tolerance and sane equanimity.

Clearly, this cultic tendency in "religion" and Spirituality, and the egoic (and, thus, cultic) tendency in life in general, must become the constant subject of fundamental human understanding—and all of humankind must constantly be put to "school", to unlearn the "method" of egocentrism, non-cooperation, intolerance, and dis-ease.

THE SUPER-PHYSICS
OF DIVINE ENLIGHTENMENT

Part Two concludes with Avatar Adi Da's description of the literal physical and psychic transformations that awaken for those who enter fully into the process of the devotional relationship to Him as Adept-Realizer—the relationship in which He instigates the Realization of Reality and Truth in His devotees.

The True Guru-Devotee Relationship Is Real Physics

Divine Self-Realization is absolutely uncommon. In Its Most Perfect Completeness, It has, until My Own Divine Avataric Appearance and Demonstration, never transpired in anyone's case in the entire history of the human "world". It is, rather, a process that belongs to the future "evolution" of humankind—at best, thousands, millions, billions of years in the future, for the human race as a whole.

At present, almost all human beings persist in an infantile developmental moment that has nothing whatsoever to do with the Ultimate Truth. As a general rule, human beings are still dependent, violent, ego-possessed—still seeking consolations in the realm of changes. Therefore, do not imagine for a moment that right and true practice of the only-by-Me Revealed and Given Reality-Way of Adidam (or Adidam Ruchiradam) is an easy matter, that you can simply Listen to My Teaching-Argument and (thereby) Realize the Intrinsically egoless and Self-Evidently Divine Self-Nature, Self-Condition, and Self-State of Reality Itself. The Reality-Way of

Adidam is the Work of Reality Itself. The Reality-Way of Adidam is the obligation (or Law) of Eternal Existence—an obligation generated, and regenerated, by the devotional relationship to Me.

The humanly incarnate Spiritual Master is Divine Help to the advantage of those in like form. When My devotee enters into right relationship with Me, changes happen in the literal physics of one's existence. I am not just talking about ideas. I am Talking about literal transformations at the level of energy, at the level of esoteric super-physics (beyond the physical limitations you characteristically presume), at the level of the Unlimited Condition of the Divine Conscious Light. That transformative process is enacted in My devotees in (and by Means of) My Divine Avataric Company.

The relationship between the Adept-Realizer and the devotee is not a matter of conceptual symbolisms or emotional attachment to some extraordinary person. The true Guru-devotee relationship is real physics. Therefore, because human beings can make unique use of the Offering of the Adept-Realizer's Company, it is to the special advantage of people when an Adept-Realizer (of whatever Real degree) appears in their midst. And that advantage is Unique in My Case, because I have Revealed and Given the <u>Complete</u> Reality-Process, Which culminates in Most Perfect (or seventh stage) Divine Self-Realization.

An Inconceivable Leap

Real Spiritual life has nothing to do with the childishness people tend to dramatize in relationship to the Spiritual Master. I Criticize that childish (or dependent) approach more directly than most people do. Others are merely petulant about the necessity of the relationship to the Spiritual Master, in the "self"-righteous mood of adolescence. Both the childish approach and the adolescent approach to the Spiritual Master are forms of destructive nonsense and must be overcome. However, the mature, ego-surrendering relationship to the Spiritual Master is absolutely Lawful and necessary. Those who object to that relationship might as well object to the relationship between the Earth and the Sun.

Most people are willing to sacrifice things, but not themselves. They are willing to pay cash, in other words, for a quick salvation. Such "religious consumerism" is an ancient ritual of worship, but it is false and futile. True worship is the surrender of your own body-mind-"self" in Truth Itself, in the Living and Transformative Company of the Spiritual Master. People absolutely resist such surrender, because they know nothing about it. Human beings are, in fact, subhuman in their present level of adaptation. Devotional surrender of the egoic "self" represents a future stage of development for humanity as a species. In their present actual, literal, psycho-physical condition, human beings are incapable of such surrender. They must be drawn out of that limited condition, and into another state of existence. And it is as far to go from where they are now to Most Perfect Divine Self-Realization as it is from the amoeba in the primal mud of the Earth to a human being. Every aspect of your existence—even the body—must change dramatically.

There is an unspeakably profound difference between the condition of the usual egoic individual and the Condition of the Divinely Enlightened individual. If imagined in "evolutionary" terms, that difference is an inconceivable leap. However, there is a Real Process for making that leap, and there is Help for it: the devotional and (in due course) Transcendental Spiritual relationship to Me, the Divine Avataric Master. In other words, something in the Super-Physics of the universe makes it possible for the Divine Conscious Light to Avatarically Incarnate as an apparent human individual, for the Purpose of Bringing others into the Sphere of Divinely Enlightened Existence. Therefore, just as the relationship to the Spiritual Master (of one or another degree) is the Supreme Principle of Spiritual life in general, the relationship to Me is the Supreme Principle of the Reality-Way of Adidam.

Divine Enlightenment
Is A Change of The <u>Whole</u> <u>Body</u>

True Spiritual life is not just a change in your mind. Much more than an "inner awakening" or a "good feeling" about everything must take place. The literal physics of your entire existence must change. The physical body and its energies must be literally transformed. Real Spiritual processes do not occur as a result of the "subjective" nonsense of vicarious belief and vicarious salvation that people usually associate with "religion"—as if Real Awakening were merely a matter of asking some silly question or going to a few lectures for the weekend.

That is not Divine Enlightenment. Divine Enlightenment is a literal change of the <u>whole</u> <u>body</u>. If you have acquired the human form, then the change that must occur in the body is not really so much in your outward appearance, because you already have the necessary structure. Rather, the changes that must occur are psycho-physical changes— just as literal as if you were to acquire more legs and arms, except that the most dramatic changes occur in dimensions other than the shape of the physical body. Changes certainly do occur in the flesh and in the elemental structures of the body, but those changes do not really alter the body's out- ward shape. Nevertheless, those changes are as literal as the "evolutionary change" from a dinosaur to a human being— and they are as dramatic as that, but they principally occur at more subtle levels of the physics of the conditional being. There are literal changes in the nervous system, literal changes in the chemistry of the body, literal changes in the structural functioning of the brain.

You cannot realize such changes in a weekend. They are a living process of growth—but they can be quickened and intensified through right practice, and real ego-transcending discipline, in My Divine Avataric Company. I Communicate My Own "Bright" Divine Self-Nature, Self-Condition, and Self-State to you, thereby Effecting a "radical" (or "at-the-root") transformation in the disposition of your body-mind-"self". And, then (over time), I Magnify the effectiveness of that disposition many times, such that the entire Process of Divine Enlightenment can, potentially, take place even in a single lifetime—or (at least) be dramatically advanced in one lifetime, if not completely fulfilled.

The Transcendental Spiritual Process in My Divine Avataric Company becomes a Perfect Self-Awakening of the whole body, through the moment to moment turning of the whole body of psycho-physical faculties to Me.* Such devotional turning to Me requires the disposition of limitless "self"-sacrifice into the Absolute Intensity of Which all conditional manifestations are stepped-down intensities (or conditionally apparent modifications). Through the by-Me-Given Process of total and complete "self"-sacrificial release into Absolute Intensity, Most Perfect Divine Self-Realization Self-Awakens. Most Perfect Divine Self-Realization is not a merely egoically-"subjective" (or bodily and mentally "internal") matter. Most Perfect Divine Self-Realization Is the Most Perfect Self-Enlightenment of the whole body. As long as the process in My Divine Avataric Company is one of growth and adaptation and purification, there is the sacrifice of the egoic "self" (or the apparently independent body-mind-complex). Most Ultimately, in the Divine Process of the seventh stage of life, the Intrinsically egoless whole body is

---

* Body, emotion, mind, and breath are the four fundamental faculties that make up the "whole body of psycho-physical faculties" of the human being. Responsive turning of those four faculties to Avatar Adi Da is the fundamental practice of the Reality-Way of Adidam.

Divinely Transfigured and Divinely Transformed—becoming (in due course) Divinely Indifferent, and (at last) Divinely Translated.*

I Show You
My Own Divine Person and Presence

In the Literature of My Divine Avataric Reality-Teaching,†
I have Described the full esoteric progression of this
remarkable Process. My Description is not based on any
mere intellectual synthesis of things I have read and thought
about. The entire process of the Reality-Way of Adidam is
My literal "Experience". My Divine Avataric Teaching-Word
brings the significance of all the patterns of existence into a
clear unity, such that the entire affair of human existence
can be approached rightly. Constant Self-Abiding As the
"Bright" (Itself) Is My Very Existence. And the Divine Avataric
Power of My Transcendental Spiritual Self-Transmission of
the "Bright" Is Available for the transformation of others—if
people will enter into devotional (and, in due course,
Transcendental Spiritual) relationship with Me.

My Own Person Is Intrinsically egoless, Transcendental
Spiritual, and Self-Evidently Divine in Nature. Some might
presume that, in order for Me to Manifest My Own Person to
them when they are at a distance from My bodily (human)
Form, it should be the case that I bilocate, that I somehow
stand in front of them in My bodily (human) Form.
However, bilocation is a phenomenon that relates to the
subtle body. What you "experience" As Me Is My Transcendental Spiritual Transmission (or Projection, or Expansion) of
My Divine Body. My Divine Body is not a physical manifestation. My Divine Body is not a subtle manifestation. I Show
you Myself—My Own Divine Person and Presence. My

* Divine Transfiguration, Divine Transformation, Divine Indifference, and Divine Translation are
the four phases of the process of the seventh stage of life in the Reality-Way of Adidam.

† To see the full range of this literature, please visit www.dawnhorsepress.com.

Divine Form Is the "Bright", the Love-Bliss-Form That you can feel Tangibly Touching you, Surrounding you, Moving in you, Making all kinds of changes. That Is My Divine Body. I can Manifest My Divine Body anywhere—and I Do So, all the time. I Only Manifest Myself.

If you enter into the devotional relationship with Me, then the Divine Process begins to duplicate Itself in your case. It is not as if you are a robot that is being transformed by some computer—no. The Process is a living and human relationship to Me. But that Process has nothing to do with the conventional "doctor-patient" and "mommy-daddy-baby" games. Irresponsible people cannot enter into this Process.

A Right and Effective Life

If you are irresponsible, you feel that you are the victim of events, the victim of your own reactivity coinciding with events. You presume that you have to analyze those events, and analyze your reactivity, and (thereby) discover what is to be blamed for your current state. Such is the "worldly" model of life, which is based entirely on the principle of egoity—and to live by that model does not lead to any real change or any real transcending of egoity. To live a right and effective life requires that you embrace the principle of responsibility—by turning whole bodily to Me, understanding your own activity of "self"-contraction, and changing your life on that basis. Past events do not control your life—you control your life. You are not a victim, and no one is to blame.

There is no event whatsoever that is so mighty that you cannot transcend your own reactivity in relation to it. None. Not one event. And not any complex of events. Moment to moment devotional turning to Me is what makes the difference. That Is the only-by-Me Revealed and Given Reality-Way of Adidam.

You must be responsible for yourself at the human level, and in a profoundly uncommon way. You must live the discipline of ordinary life. You yourself must be love under all ordinary, daily conditions. You must make this change in your life. There is no way whereby you can be relieved of this necessity—and nobody else can do it for you. Nevertheless, all of that ordinary responsibility simply prepares you for the right relationship to Me (in and As My Divinely-Avatarically-Born bodily human Divine Form and Person).

An Advantage
Unique In Human Time

I Am your Unique Advantage, because I Am Present in the same kind of bodily form as you—Manifested via the same kind of physical structure, the same kind of nervous system, the same kind of brain. In My Case, however, all these mechanisms are Conformed to an Absolute level of Functioning, such that your entering into Communion with Me brings changes even at the level of the psycho-physical body that you present to Me.

No abstract Divine Principle can serve you in that manner—because the physics of this Process must be directly Present, and the bodily (human) Demonstration of the Process must be Present in a Form that can Do Its Work in your case. That Work Is My Purpose. My Divine Avataric Self-Incarnation Fully Manifests the State of the Ultimate Physics of things—Which is your Potential, but not your actuality at the present time. The "abstract Divine" and the powers of the universe are not (in and of themselves) organized for the sake of the immediate transformation of human beings. If people truly enter into right devotional and (in due course) Transcendental Spiritual relationship with Me, they will (inevitably) Realize the process of transformation characteristic of the only-by-Me Revealed and Given Reality-Way of Adidam.

I Am here to Reveal the Perfect Teaching of Truth Itself and to Initiate the great culture of compassion and Wisdom among human beings. However, those Purposes are secondary aspects of My Divine Avataric Service to humanity. Those Purposes are the Transformative Effects of My "Bright" Divine State and My Ultimate Divine Function. My True and Ultimate Divine Avataric Function Is to Instigate the Super-Physics of Most Perfect Real-God-Realization (or Divine Enlightenment) among My true devotees.

My Avataric Self-Manifestation in bodily (human) Divine Form Is an Advantage That Is Unique in human time.

The Connection with the Divine
Is _Perfectly_ _Prior_.
The Connection with the Divine
Is _Always_ _Already_ _The_ _Case_.

The "distance" is vanished.
The separation is vanished.

There is no "problem".
There is no separation.
No "method" is required.
No seeking is instigated.

My Divine Avataric Gift Is Full.
My Divine Avataric Gift Is everywhere—
for everyone.

AVATAR ADI DA SAMRAJ

THE REALITY-WAY
I OFFER TO EVERYONE

THERE IS ONE TRUTH—
WHICH IS ALWAYS ALREADY
THE CASE

Part Three begins with a consideration Avatar Adi Da often used to help people understand the relationship between their own experience of existence and His Revelation of Reality Itself: the room as it appears and the room as it is.

1.

The "world" is not as you perceive the "world" to be, nor as you think the "world" to be, nor as you describe the "world" to be. You do not perceive the "world" As it Is. You perceive the "world" from the "point of view" of your own "location" in time and space.

2.

You can vouch for something about what the apparent room looks like from where you are sitting right now, from the perspective of your eyes, and mind, and perception altogether. You have a perceived "location". You see the room in that mode. You could describe the room at great length— but you would still not be seeing the room As it Is. What does the room actually look like? You never see the totality of the room.

If each person's "point of view" were replaced by a camera, and you collected photographs of all those "points of view" in the room—up, down, sides, all different orientations— and if you put them all together, you would wonder what you were looking at. Ten such photographs would be enough to make the room unrecognizable. In any case, no single photograph represents the room in its totality. Any single photograph is a portrayal (or an abstract representation) only—and the same is true of your perception. Your perception is only a portrayal (or an abstract representation) of the room. Your perception is not the room As it Is.

3.

What, in fact, does the universe look like from every possible "point of view" in (and beyond) space and time? "Real God" is as good a term as any to describe this "look". To recognize the universe in its Indivisibility, and (otherwise) in its Totality—beyond description, beyond time, and beyond place—is to "Know" the universe in the Divine sense. There is no doubt about the existence of the universe, regardless of how much you "know" or do not "know" about it.

4.

Describing the room As it Is is the same as describing Truth Itself, or Reality Itself. Consciousness Itself—the "Bright", the Divine Conscious Light, the Self-Existing and Self-Radiant Reality—is not merely the "inward" core of the ego-"I". Truth Itself, or Reality Itself, is not "subjective" in the egoic sense. The Truth is not—and cannot be—attained or Realized by means of the mechanisms of the body-mind-complex. Only in the intrinsic and Perfect transcending of the mechanisms of the body-mind-complex, only in the intrinsic and total transcending of all the "methods", and all the naive "religions" (or "tribal" mythologies), and all the searches built upon the mechanism of the body-mind-complex—

indeed, only in the intrinsic and Perfect transcending of "point of view" itself—is there Ultimacy. Such is the only-by-Me Revealed and Given seventh stage Way of Reality-Realization.

5.

There Is One Truth, One Ultimate and Most Perfect Realization. It Is the Realization of That Which Is Always Already The Case. It is not you (or the "I" to which you refer) that will Realize What Is. The Realization of Reality Itself is not a "you"-versus-"object" process or result.

The room (or conditional reality) exists. Real (Acausal) God Exists. Ultimately, they are Realized to Be the Same. Reality Is Real God. Reality Is What the room Is, What anything Is, What anyone Is. Reality Is Who Is. Reality is not "you" in the "inside-of-the-ego" sense. Reality is not merely the platform of separateness, not merely the awareness that looks at the feeling of relatedness. The Reality to be Realized Is Transcendental Spiritual in Nature. The Reality to be Realized Is Incomprehensible, Beyond definition. Nevertheless, Reality Is Realizable—As My Divine Avataric Gift.

In Reality Itself, the ego has no relevance whatsoever—none. In Reality Itself, the ego has no existence. In Reality Itself, there is nothing but the Divine "Bright" Spherical Self-Domain*—Which has not been described, indicated, or Realized in the entire history of the Great Tradition of humankind.

---

* Here, Avatar Adi Da is affirming a Divine "Domain" that is the True Condition of the conditional worlds. It is not "elsewhere", nor an "objective place" (like a subtle "heaven" or mythical "paradise"). Rather, It is the evidently Divine Condition or Context of every conditionally manifested being and thing. Avatar Adi Da Reveals more fully in His other writings that this Divine Self-Domain can be described as a Boundless (and Boundlessly "Bright") Sphere of Conscious Light.

REALITY IS INHERENTLY FREE

In the ecstasy of His spontaneous speech, Avatar Adi Da poetically describes the Divinely Enlightened Realization of Reality and Truth.

1.

The Inherent Self-Radiance
of Being
Is Bliss,
Freedom,
Happiness,
Fullness,
Non-conditional Well-Being.

This Is
Inherently The Case—
not merely the case
sometimes,
somewhere else,
after death.

The Inherent Self-Radiance
of Being
Is the Condition
of existence.
Therefore,
the Integrity of Being
is to Realize This,
Always Already.

And Real practice is
everything in a life
done to Realize This,
Always Already—
until It Is
Self-Evidently Realized,
Always Already.

And then
There Is
Just That.
And That
Is That.

2.

It is not that
you are the body,
and that,
by going "deeper",
you discover
that the "deeper" part of you
is Consciousness.

No—
You Stand
As Consciousness.
And That Is
Self-Evident.
No matter what arises
(or does not arise),
you Are That.
That Is simply The Case.

3.

I <u>Am</u>
the Room.
And
I <u>Am</u>
the Light within It.

There is
no "inside",
and
no "outside".

There Is
simply
the Self-Existing,
Self-Radiant
Sphere
of
Consciousness Itself.

No "subject",
no "object",
no familiarity.

No separation,
no "difference".

No "problem".

Inherent
Integrity and Fullness
of Being.

Perfect
Equanimity
of View.

This very room is not familiar.
It is an unfamiliar place.

Where is this?
And who are you?

There is no "you"
about it.
It is Obvious
What Is.

There is no need
to make reference
to any separate one—
except that,
for convenience,
names are given
to each body
(or bodily presence)
in the pattern,
without confusing
bodily existence
with the Condition
of Reality,
Which Is Inherently Free.

Therefore,
all the while,
with all the names and forms,
There Is
This Inherent

Unfamiliarity
of Fullness,
of Consciousness Itself—
the Current of Being Itself,
a Sphere of Being,
Self-Lit,
in Which all forms appear
as modifications
of the Inherent Light.

But,
from the "Disposition"
of the Inherent Light
(or Consciousness Itself),
there are
no things,
no changes.

4.

The Process Goes On
until It Is Most Full,
Most Perfect.

There are
conditional
glimpses,
tastes,
changes,
and so forth,
in the course of ego-transcending practice.

The Realization Itself
Is Beyond
all of that.

REALITY IS REALIZABLE

In these selections from a longer talk, Avatar Adi Da speaks of the Nature of Reality Itself and how the devotional relationship to Him provides a unique means for Realizing It.

The Reality-Condition Is Sitting Before Your Eyes

The Position of Reality Itself Is the Position of and <u>As</u> That Which Is Always Already The Case.

Reality Itself <u>Is</u> <u>So</u> now.

Most Ultimately, Reality Itself will be Realized to Be So, and to have Always Already Been So.

Reality Itself Is the Context of <u>all</u> "experiencing".

Reality Itself Is Truth.

Reality Itself Is What is to be Realized—not merely eventually, but always immediately, directly, and tacitly.

That Reality Itself <u>Is</u> Truth Is the Realization Sitting before you, in My Own Person.

The Divine Reality-Way of Adidam is <u>Self</u>-Revealed, in Person, before your eyes.

I <u>Am</u> That Which is to Be Realized.

The Reality-Condition, Self-Revealed to you, must be entered into profoundly—Such That "It" is Realized now and <u>As</u> "It" <u>Is</u>.

The Reality-Condition could be Realized simply by Sighting Me here, in My Divinely-Avatarically-Born bodily (human) Divine Form.

My "Bright" Divine Self-Nature, Self-Condition, and Self-State could be immediately Obvious to you.

The reason that My "Bright" Divine Self-Nature, Self-Condition, and Self-State is <u>not</u> Obvious to you is that you are bound up in your own errors, your own habits, your own "self"-reflection, your own egoic "self"-identification with the body-mind-complex.

The "Bright" Divine State of Reality Itself Is always First, always the Basis of all "experience".

That State is not the condition of bondage in which you characteristically presume to exist.

Reality Itself Is Perfectly Obvious (or Always Already Self-Evident).

Reality Itself is not subject to doubt.

Yet, you dismiss Reality Itself—moment to moment.

<u>Only</u> Reality Itself Is Always Already The Case.

What "It" <u>Is</u> must be Realized—by entering into "It" profoundly.

Reality Itself Is the "Root"-Condition, or Source-Condition, of all-and-All.

Reality and Conditions
Are Not Equivalent

Your Real Status Is That of Consciousness Itself—Which is not "causing" (or even doing) anything whatsoever, Which is not watching (or observing) in any conditional sense, Which has no psycho-physical identity, Which Is Inherently Free of all such identity, Which has no involvement in "self"-contraction whatsoever, for Which there is no body-mind-"self", for Which there are no gross, subtle, or causal* dimensions of conditional existence, for Which there is no conditional existence whatsoever, no cosmic domain, no "world", no limitation.

---

* Avatar Adi Da (in agreement with certain traditional esoteric schools) describes conditional existence as having three fundamental dimensions: gross (material or physical, associated with the physical body and the waking state), subtle (etheric, associated with the lower and higher mental functions and the dreaming state), and causal (the "root" of attention, associated with the state of deep sleep).

Consciousness Itself Is Inherently Free and Inherently Perfect.

Consciousness Itself Is Self-Existing and Self-Radiant.

Consciousness Itself is not "within" you.

Consciousness Itself is not "behind" the body-mind-"self", or "deep in" the body-mind-"self".

It is not that you, as My devotee, must progress through the body-mind-complex, in order to discover Consciousness Itself when you get to the end of the potentials of the body-mind. That notion of the Way is an ego-based metaphor for a Way to Reality that is created by the body-mind's perspective (or "point of view").

The body-mind-complex is not the means (or the connection) to Reality Itself (or the Divine Self-Nature, Self-Condition, and Self-State Itself).

Reality Itself Is Self-Existing and Self-Radiant—Always Already The Case.

Most Perfect Divine Self-Realization Is Prior Realization of That Which Is Always Already The Case.

Most Perfect Divine Self-Realization is not the result of a process in which you are being non-Realization and looking toward Realization.

Most Perfect Divine Self-Realization is not a result of working toward Reality.

Most Perfect Divine Self-Realization is not a matter of progressively eliminating anything, or "causing" anything, or proceeding toward a goal.

Most Perfect Divine Self-Realization Is As Is—Just So, Priorly, Perfectly, and Always Already.

Most Perfect Divine Self-Realization Is (Inherently) Most Perfect renunciation, because Realization is Always Already not identified with the body-mind-"self".

There is no equation between Reality Itself and conditional appearances—no equation whatsoever.

Reality Itself is not the "Creator" (or "Cause") of conditions.

The Status of conditions Is Self-Evident when there is Most Perfect Divine Self-Realization of Reality Itself.

I <u>Am</u> That Which is to be Realized.

Truth Without Medium

I have Revealed the Truth—and I <u>Am</u> the Revelation of the Truth.

I <u>Am</u> That Truth.

The Truth is Given by Me, Directly.

The Truth is Given by Me without transition, without medium, without "cause".

I am not here to "<u>cause</u>" Realization in you.

I <u>Am</u> the Acausal and Most Perfect Realization of the Truth That <u>Is</u> Reality Itself.

Therefore, you must recognize Me—and, by your devotional response to Me, be utterly given to Me, such that you (Ultimately) Realize Me Most Perfectly.

In Most Perfect Realization of Me, there is not a trace of egoity, not a trace of status, not a trace of body-mind-"self". Realization of Me has no content or status whatsoever. There is nothing to claim in Most Perfect Realization of Me. To Realize My "Bright" Divine Self-Nature, Self-Condition, and Self-State is to be Lost in the Divine, Found in the Divine, Relieved of all seeking, Relieved of all transitions, all means, all purpose.

REALITY ITSELF
IS AT THE BEGINNING

*Avatar Adi Da describes His Work as being for everyone—
beyond the cultural traditions of both East and West. Anyone
can practice the Reality-Way He has Given, because it is
founded in Truth Itself.*

1.

I am not merely on one "tribal" side or another.
I Transcend all—and I Include all.
My Divine Avataric Revelation-Teaching is Offered to everyone—as Universal and Unique Wisdom That Cuts Through the limitations in everyone, without selectivity.

I cannot be compartmentalized as a Westerner, or as an Easterner, or as a Hindu, or as a non-Hindu, or as a Buddhist, or as a non-Buddhist, or as a Christian, or as a non-Christian, or as a "whatever".

I am not anything but Myself—Standing Prior to all-and-All.

I <u>Am</u> the Divine Avatar—Transcending both East and West.

I <u>Am</u> the Truth of Reality Itself.

I Stand Prior to all-and-All—and I Transcend all-and-All.

2.

The Divine Reality-Truth is <u>never</u>, Itself, limited and defined by any circumstance of appearances. Conditions may "experientially" (and, thus, conditionally) arise and appear—but <u>all</u> "experiential" appearances are merely apparent modifications of the Intrinsically egoless, Perfectly

Indivisible, Perfectly Acausal, and Ever-Free Divine and Transcendental Spiritual Conscious Light That Is Reality Itself. That One Conscious Light of all-and-All Is Reality-Truth.

If apparent conditions are not Divinely Self-Recognized, then they are tacitly granted a power to apparently define the Divine Reality-Truth as limited, confined, and motivated by presently-arising appearances.

If apparent conditions are Divinely Self-Recognized, then that power is not granted to apparent conditions, and the otherwise inevitable struggle with conditions is (thus and thereby) undermined and vanished at its "root".

You are tending to live a life of struggle, seeking to attain equilibrium, pleasure, or release—either in the present "world" or in some other "world". However, this struggle is unnecessary—if only you will (Intrinsically, tacitly, in moment to moment recognition-responsive* devotional Communion with Me) transcend (and, in that tacit sense, understand) the gesture of "self"-contraction in the apparent field of the body-mind-complex and its relations.

Such is the necessary "radical" (or always "at-the-root", and not mentally proposed, or mind-driven and search-oriented) "self"-understanding—or Intrinsic transcending of psycho-physical "self"-contraction—that is always already (tacitly, and Priorly) founded in the Divine Reality-Truth.

3.

The only-by-Me Revealed and Given Reality-Way of Adidam (or Adidam Ruchiradam) Is a Perfect Revelation—Free of all limiting associations.

---

* Here Avatar Adi Da is referring to the foundation of the Reality-Way of Adidam He offers: the direct and wordless "Locating" and "Knowing" of Him as the "Bright" (or Reality Itself), Avatarically Appearing in bodily (human) Form. When there is such devotional recognition of Avatar Adi Da Samraj, there is inevitably the simultaneous impulse to devotionally respond to Him. The entire practice of the Reality-Way of Adidam is founded in this recognition-response to Avatar Adi Da Samraj.

The Teaching of the Reality-Way of Adidam always and inherently relieves people of whatever they are struggling to defend.

The Teaching of the Reality-Way of Adidam does not call upon the machinery of defensiveness.

The Teaching of the Reality-Way of Adidam is not a "something" over against a "something else".

The Teaching of the Reality-Way of Adidam Stands Prior to everything (so-called) "else".

The Teaching of the Reality-Way of Adidam calls upon everyone's tacit sense of That Which Is Truth Itself, Reality Itself, the True and Perfect Divine.

4.

Anyone can practice the only-by-Me Revealed and Given Reality-Way of Adidam, because the Reality-Way of Adidam Is Prior to all limitations.

Anyone can respond to Me directly and immediately. That is why the practice of the Reality-Way of Adidam is effective. That is why devotion to Me is fundamental.

No "great path of return"* is required in order to enter into the Divine Reality-Way of Adidam.

The only-by-Me Revealed and Given Divine Reality-Way of Adidam simply involves direct, and whole bodily, and recognition-responsive devotional turning to Me.

Right and true devotional turning to Me utterly bypasses (and, thus, intrinsically transcends) whatever ego-bondage is the case for any individual.

Therefore, anyone can directly and immediately respond to Me and take up the "Radical" Reality-Way of Adidam— because it does not require going through a "great path of return" in order to do so.

---

* The "great path of return" is Avatar Adi Da's term for the traditional search to "return" to the Divine Reality by means of a strategic effort.

5.

The "Radical" Reality-Way of Adidam is about the tacit, searchless, and Intrinsic transcending of both "self" and not-"self" in Intrinsically egoless, Perfectly Indivisible, Perfectly Acausal, and Self-Evidently Divine Reality Itself— Which Was and Is before anyone's search (or even any culture's "religion") begins.

The Always Already Self-Presence of Reality Itself Is the Secret upon Which right and true practice of the only-by-Me Revealed and Given "Radical" Reality-Way of Adidam Is Founded.

The only-by-Me Revealed and Given "Radical" Reality-Way of Adidam Is the Divine and Prior and Perfect and Complete Way of Reality Itself.

6.

Reality Itself does not come only at the end of the "Radical" Reality-Way of Adidam.

Reality Itself Is at the beginning of the "Radical" Reality-Way of Adidam.

Therefore, Reality Itself does not require that you first work through a seeking-process of "evolving" your egoic "self" before Intrinsically egoless Reality Itself is available and accessible As the Principle of practice.

Reality Itself Is the Divine Acausal Means of Realization and Liberation.

Reality Itself Is the only-by-Me Revealed and Given Divine and "Radical" Reality-Way of Adidam—or Adidam Ruchiradam.

WHAT I BRING TO HERE

In this concluding essay, Avatar Adi Da Offers to all His Gift of the direct Revelation of Truth Itself.

1.

What I Bring to here Is the Divine Avataric Self-Revelation of Reality Itself.
What I Bring to here Is the Absolute Divine Itself, Self-Revealed.
What I Bring to here is not mythology.
What I Bring to here is not "religion".
What I Bring to here is not anything that human beings already "know".
What I Bring to here is not a path or a search that is already evident in the history of the Great Tradition of humankind.
What I Bring to here has never been offered before, never heard of before, never practiced before.

2.

This Divine Avataric Self-Revelation of the Obvious can only be Given As a Gift—because, by seeking the Truth, humankind only wanders from It.

3.

Therefore—now, and forever hereafter—What I Offer you is simply My Divine Avataric Company.

Whether or not you are in proximity to My physical human Body, The Offering of My Divine Avataric Company is extended to you in every moment.

4.

I Offer <u>Only</u> The Direct Self-Revelation of Reality Itself.

No "answers" that could be given to your "questions"— and no "techniques" (or ego-based seeking-"methods", or "prescriptions for remedy") that could be given to you to practice—are relevant to Reality-Realization.

5.

The Realization of The Truth of Reality Itself cannot be "caused"—but "It" can (and, indeed, must) Be Given.

6.

My Offering is here for <u>all</u>.

7.

Accept My "Bright" Gift
Of Perfectly egoless
Conscious Light
and
Of Divine
Transcendental Spiritual
Love-Bliss.

Avatar Adi Da Samraj
Adi Da Samrajashram, 2008

EPILOGUE

FALL INTO
MY HEART

FALL INTO MY HEART

You become (or take the form of) what your attention most really moves upon.

Therefore, if I Am your Beloved, your love-attention for Me allows you to Realize Indivisible Unity with Me—moment to moment, in every now of time and space.

Until you fall in love, love is what you fear to do.

When you have fallen in love, and you are (thus) always already in love, then you cease to fear to love—you cease to be reluctant to surrender, and you cease to be reluctant to be "self"-forgetful and foolish, and to be single-minded, and to suffer an "other".

Those who fall in love with Me, Fall into Me.

Those whose hearts are given, in love, to Me, Fall into My Heart.

Those who are Mine, because they are in love with Me, no longer demand to be fulfilled through conditional "experience" and through the survival (or perpetuation) of the ego-"I".

Their love for Me grants them Access to Me, and (Thus) to My Love-Bliss—because I Am the Divine Love-Bliss, in Person.

What will My devotee do but love Me?

I suffer every form and condition of every one who loves Me, because I Love My devotee As My Own Form, My Own Condition.

I Love My devotee As the One by Whom I Am Distracted.

I Grant all My Own Divine and "Bright" Excesses to those who love Me, in exchange for all their doubts and sufferings.

Those who "Bond" themselves to Me, through love-surrender, are inherently Free of fear and wanting need.

They transcend the ego-"I" (the "cause" of all conditional "experience"), and they ("cause", and all, and All) Dissolve in Me—for I Am the Heart of all-and-All, and I Am the Heart Itself, and the Heart Itself Is the "causeless", and egoless, and Perfectly Only Reality, Truth, and Real God of all-and-All.

What is a Greater Message than This?

Sources of the Selections
in *The Gift of Truth Itself*

Essays from *The Aletheon* that are included in full are indicated with a bullet point (•) and retain their original titles, as given by Adi Da Samraj. All other essays, except where noted, are compilations or excerpts of essays from *The Aletheon*, and were given new titles, derived from Avatar Adi Da's own language, by the editors. All books indicated in this list are published by the Dawn Horse Press (Middletown, CA).

PROLOGUE

From a discourse given by Avatar Adi Da on December 20, 1998, published in *Notice This*.

PART ONE

Facing quotation
From "Eleutherios", Part Four of *The Gnosticon*.

Truth and Reality Can Be Neither Proven Nor Disproven
Selected passages from "The Criticism That Cures The Heart", in Part Two of *The Aletheon*.

Truth Is Not A Mere Social Gospel
Selected passages from "The Dogmas of Social Morality Versus The Esoteric Spiritual Teaching That Is At The Origin of Traditional Religions", in Part Two of *The Aletheon* (section titles supplied by the editors).

• The Western Prohibition Against Higher Knowledge and Realization Versus The Eastern Advocacy of Higher Knowledge and Realization
From Part Two of *The Aletheon* (section titles supplied by the editors).

Child-Made Awareness of Reality
From "The Parental Deity and The One To Be Realized", in Part Two of *The Aletheon*.

The Childish Presumption of "God-Apart" and The Adolescent Presumption of "Separate self"
Selected passages from "Moving Beyond Childish and Adolescent Approaches To Life and Truth", in Part Two of *The Aletheon*.

• God As The Creator, God As Good, and God As The Real
From Part Two of *The Aletheon* (section titles supplied by the editors).

• Tacit Certainty of Real God
From Part Two of *The Aletheon*.

PART TWO

Facing quotation
From "True Devotion Is Perfect Knowledge Demonstrated By Renunciation", in Part Ten of *The Aletheon*.

• Adept-Realizers Are The Root of All Esoteric Traditions
From Part Three of *The Aletheon*.

• The Great Esoteric Tradition of Devotion To The Adept-Realizer
From Part Three of *The Aletheon* (section titles supplied by the editors).

• Beyond The Cultic Tendency In Religion and Spirituality, and In Secular Society
From Part Three of *The Aletheon*.

• The Super-Physics of Divine Enlightenment
From Part Three of *The Aletheon* (section titles supplied by the editors).

PART THREE

Facing quotation
From "The Boundless Self-Confession", Part Twenty-Four of *The Aletheon*.

There Is One Truth—Which Is Always Already The Case
Selected passages from "The Way of Zero Bargaining", in Part Seventeen of *The Aletheon*.

Reality Is Inherently Free
Selected passages from "Most Perfect Divine Self-Awakening To The Domain of Conscious Light", in Part Seventeen of *The Aletheon*.

Reality Is Realizable
Selected passages from "The Way of Zero Bargaining", in Part Seventeen of *The Aletheon* (section titles supplied by the editors).

Reality Itself Is At The Beginning
Selected passages from "The Divine Reality-Way", in Part Four of *The Aletheon*.

What I Bring To Here
Selected passages from *The Aletheon* (Section 1: From "There Is A Way—and Reality Itself Is It", in Part Twenty-One; Section 2: From "The Meditative and The Sacramental Forms of Devotional Communion With Me", in Part Nine; Sections 3–4: From "Radical Adidam", in Part Eight; Section 5: From "Perfect Dis-Illusionment", in Part Eight; Section 6: From "The Way of Zero Bargaining", in Part Seventeen; Section 7: From "Hridaya Rosary", Part Thirteen).

EPILOGUE

From "What Is A Greater Message Than This?", Part Twenty-Six of *The Aletheon*.

Avatar Adi Da Samraj
Adi Da Samrajashram, 2008

The Universal Offering

of

Avatar Adi Da Samraj

THE UNIVERSAL OFFERING
OF AVATAR ADI DA SAMRAJ

by

Ruchiradama Quandra Sukhapur Rani Naitauba

(on behalf of the Ruchira Sannyasin Order of Adidam Ruchiradam*)

In response to all the human voices calling out to the Divine, Avatar Adi Da Samraj took Birth on Earth, in bodily (human) Form, in November 1939. In His sixtieth year, His Divine Avataric Incarnation culminated in the most consequential Event ever to occur in the cosmic domain: In April 2000, His Holy Body was Divinely Translated, becoming the utterly transparent Doorway to the Divine Domain of Reality Itself. After that supremely consequential Event, His Divine Body and Life became as if ash from a sacred fire, and His Body Stood as the Universal Channel of connection to the Divine, Perfectly.

In His Divine Avataric Lifetime, Avatar Adi Da Samraj had a Single Purpose, which was to re-connect all cosmic worlds to That Which Is Reality Itself, or Truth at the "root", prior to any separate identity in time or space. The vast undifferentiated field of Divine Conscious Light was His only Awareness. In His Awareness, there were no separate beings. Only all beings were there, in prior unity—to be Awakened and re-connected to the Infinite Truth of existence. In His Divine Avataric Lifetime, Avatar Adi Da Established the Eternal Means for the Perfect Awakening of all beings—and then, on November 27, 2008, Outshined even His own Bodily

---

* The senior renunciate order in Adidam Ruchiradam is the Ruchira Sannyasin Order. Devotees in the Ruchira Sannyasin Order have chosen to consecrate their lives utterly to Avatar Adi Da and the Reality-Way He Gives by embracing the life of formal and legal renunciation, in the circumstance of perpetual retreat.

Incarnation, in the Perfect "Brightness" of His Divine Mahasamadhi.* Now Avatar Adi Da Exists in His Eternal Form for all time. Avatar Adi Da Appeared in human Form for a time, in order to Reveal His Divine Form—thus tangibly Manifesting His Divine Transcendental Spiritual Presence, so that His Blessing-Transmission could be Perpetually Alive and Always Blessing all. This was His Divine Purpose.

Throughout His human Lifetime, Avatar Adi Da Samraj established "Channels", or "Agents", through which His Communication and Transmission of Reality-Truth would forever flow. During His Lifetime, Avatar Adi Da wrote an extraordinary number of books of the most pristine Transcendental Spiritual Revelation and esoteric Instruction ever revealed—books that infuse the heart and mind with overwhelming "Perfect Knowledge" and profoundest "Brightening" Force. Avatar Adi Da created a vast body of groundbreaking artwork—including paintings, drawings, photographic work, video work, and digitally-created work (in both two and three dimensions)—artwork which conveys His Liberating Message in a non-verbal form which He called "Transcendental Realism". Avatar Adi Da also created "Transcendental Realist" theatre, as a means of enabling a "performance-assisted subjective process" that actually leads to a transformation of the being for anyone who engages the performance in a fully participatory manner. Avatar Adi Da also Spiritually Empowered Hermitages and Sanctuaries in different parts of the world—places from which His Blessing Radiates with unique potency, now and forever. Avatar Adi Da bequeathed to humankind the entire legacy of His Divine Life-History—all of the Divine Yogic stories of everything He did and of His constant Liberating Work with those who came to Him. And Avatar Adi Da also undertook a comprehensive inspection of the Great Tradition of humankind, creating *The Basket of Tolerance*, His Supreme Clarifying

---

* In Sanskrit, "Maha" means "great" and "samadhi" means "exalted State"—and "mahasamadhi" is a traditional reference to the physical death of a Realizer.

Revelation relative to all human endeavor—religious, Spiritual, philosophical, artistic, and practical. All of these Divine Gifts of Transcendental Spiritual Revelation are "Doorways" created by the Divine Avatar, Adi Da Samraj, through which human beings can enter into "egoless participation in Reality Itself".

In the last years of His Life, Avatar Adi Da Gave a unique Gift to the human family—His description of how the human sphere of strife and conflict can be transformed into a world of cooperation, tolerance, and peace. In His book *Not-Two Is Peace*, Avatar Adi Da calls for the creation of a "Global Cooperative Forum", in which all of the people on Earth—or, in His words, "everybody-all-at-once"—are enabled to embrace an absolutely necessary paradigm shift—the shift from competition and conflict to living as an "egoless collective". Such egoless participation (by "everybody-all-at-once") is how He says we will save the Earth from destruction.

Avatar Adi Da's ultimate Gift to all is the Divine Way of life He Revealed. He named that Way of life "Adidam"—or, in its fullest form, "the 'Radical' Reality-Way of Adidam Ruchiradam". That Way is "Radical" because it goes straight to the "root" of all human problem and suffering and Reveals What Is Prior. That Way is only about Reality—not about any kind of belief, mythology, or dogma, and not about any kind of seeking-effort.

The Reality-Way of Adidam Ruchiradam is the Supreme Divine Way. It has never been given before Avatar Adi Da's Divine Birth and His Divine Work. Avatar Adi Da's Universal Offering Transcends the entire Great Tradition of humankind, and Avatar Adi Da Samraj Himself now Stands As the "Threshold Personality", making it possible for all to Awaken to That Which Is the Real, His Eternal Divine Form. ∎

Om Sri Parama-Sapta-Na Adi Da Love-Ananda Samraj

To find Avatar Adi Da Samraj is to find the Very Heart of Reality—tangibly Known, Prior to body and mind, as the Deepest Truth of existence. This is the Great Mystery that Avatar Adi Da Samraj Revealed through His Avataric Lifetime, and the Great Mystery that is forever to be discovered.

Avatar Adi Da Samraj established many ways in which people can enter into relationship with His Eternal Being. In establishing these forms of relationship, Avatar Adi Da accounted for people in all walks of life, people in all parts of the world, and people either with or without a religious practice. All of these forms of relationship to Avatar Adi Da are ways of entering into egoless participation in Reality Itself.

All beings have already been Divinely Touched by His Person, and all can therefore connect to His Eternal Divine Form, through the many ways of relating to Avatar Adi Da that He created for the sake of all, during His Divine Incarnation on Earth.

■ Avatar Adi Da established two formal renunciate orders for those who are, by Divine Grace, most seriously impulsed to Realization of the Divine Reality Itself.

The senior renunciate order is the Ruchira Sannyasin Order. Devotees in the Ruchira Sannyasin Order take a vow of full formal renunciation (or sannyas) by which they renounce all ownership of property, and (more profoundly) renounce all social ego-identity. Ruchira Sannyasin devotees embrace a life entirely devoted to the process of Divine Self-Realization, living on perpetual retreat at one of the Hermitages or Sanctuaries Empowered by Avatar Adi Da (as a general rule, at His principal Hermitage, Adi Da Samrajashram).

The second formal renunciate order is the Lay Renunciate Order, whose members serve under the governance and direction of the Ruchira Sannyasin Order. Lay Renunciate devotees are given over to serve the culture of Adidam Ruchiradam and the bringing of Avatar Adi Da's Revelation to the world—living wherever it is necessary to serve Avatar Adi Da's Revelation-Work for the sake of all beings.

■ Avatar Adi Da established a form of devotional practice for those who are moved by profound response to Avatar Adi Da, and thus are moved to dedicate their lives to Avatar Adi Da through heart-felt service and the embrace of a simple and purifying life of practice. This form of practice was Blessed by Avatar Adi Da to be the lifelong practice engaged by great numbers of people, including specific forms of participation for children and young people. And this form of practice is also the necessary foundation for those who are moved to enter the renunciate orders.

■ Avatar Adi Da established a form of devotional practice for those who are moved to support His Great Divine Avataric Work through advocacy, patronage, scholarly communication, and other forms of service. This form of practice is open to all who are moved to it, whether or not they are already involved in another religious practice.

■ Avatar Adi Da established a form of devotional practice for people who live in any of the traditional (or indigenous) cultures throughout the world. This form of practice is also open to all who are moved to it, whether or not they are already involved in the traditional religious practice of their culture (or any other religious practice).

■ Finally, Avatar Adi Da established a Calling to all beings to participate in bringing into being a Global Cooperative Forum, based on the prior unity of the entire human family. This shift in the global life of humankind is of the profoundest significance for the future of the Earth and all its inhabitants. Avatar Adi Da's Calling for the Global Cooperative Forum is presented online at:

www.da-peace.org

The Sacred Literature
of
Avatar Adi Da Samraj

THE GREAT REVELATION-BOOKS

The Aletheon is Avatar Adi Da's paramount Scripture—a pure exposition of His own Revelation, which He calls the "Seventh Way" (in reference to His schema of seven stages of life). In *The Gnosticon* and *The Pneumaton*, Avatar Adi Da examines the methods of the greatest traditions of human Spirituality and Transcendental Realization, in light of the Transcendental Spirituality of the Reality-Way of Adidam. These three Revelation-Books together form a guide to the "radical" means of the Realization of Reality and an all-encompassing Address to the entire history of human religious and Spiritual endeavor. *The Dawn Horse Testament* is Avatar Adi Da's summary of the entire seventh stage Reality-Way of Adidam.

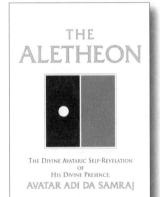

THE DIVINE AVATARIC SELF-REVELATION
OF
HIS DIVINE PRESENCE,
AVATAR ADI DA SAMRAJ

THE ALETHEON
The Divine Avataric Self-Revelation of His Divine Presence, Avatar Adi Da Samraj

Avatar Adi Da's Completing exposition of the "Seventh Stage" Way of Adidam Ruchiradam.

2322 pp.
$180 (eight-volume softcover set in slipcase)
$250 (single-volume hardcover in slipcase)

THE GNOSTICON

The "Perfect Knowledge" Reality-Teachings of His Divine Presence, Avatar Adi Da Samraj

Avatar Adi Da's examination of the Transcendental Teachings of the Great Adept-Realizers and the Transcendental Spiritual Reality-Way of Adidam Ruchiradam.

1186 pp.

$75.00 (softcover), **$150.00** (hardcover)

THE PNEUMATON

The Transcendental Spiritual Reality-Teachings of His Divine Presence, Avatar Adi Da Samraj

Avatar Adi Da's discussion of the devotional and Spiritual traditions of humankind—particularly as seen in Christianity and Hinduism—and the Transcendental Spiritual Reality-Way of Adidam Ruchiradam.

1346 pp.

$75.00 (softcover), **$175.00** (hardcover)

THE DAWN HORSE TESTAMENT

The "Testament of Secrets" of His Divine Presence, Avatar Adi Da Samraj

In *The Dawn Horse Testament*, Avatar Adi Da gives a complete summary of the entire Reality-Way of Adidam—flowing seamlessly from His Self-Revelation in the opening sections; through a "consideration" of His Life and Work, expositions of His fundamental Teaching-Arguments and the core practices He gives to His devotees, and incisive descriptions of the egoic patterns of individual beings and human collectives; through the course of the demonstration of the Reality-Way of Adidam, culminating in seventh stage Divine Enlightenment; to the declaration of the Establishment of the Realization of the "Bright" and the Perpetual Revelation of the "Bright" via the Agency of His Work and Word and Person. New edition forthcoming.

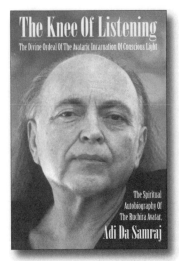

THE KNEE OF LISTENING

The Divine Ordeal of The Avataric Incarnation of Conscious Light

The Spiritual Autobiography of Avatar Adi Da Samraj

Born in 1939 on Long Island, New York, Adi Da Samraj describes His earliest Life as an existence of constant and unmitigated Spiritual "Brightness". His observation, still in infancy, that others did not live in this manner led Him to undertake an awesome quest—to discover why human beings suffer and how they can transcend that suffering. His quest led Him to a confrontation with the bleak despair of post-industrial Godlessness, to a minute examination of the workings of subjective awareness, to discipleship in a lineage of profound Yogis, to a period of intense Christian mysticism, and finally to a Re-Awakening to the perfect state of "Brightness" He had known at Birth.

In *The Knee of Listening*, Avatar Adi Da also reveals His own direct awareness of His "deeper-personality vehicles"—the beings whose lives were the direct antecedents (or the "pre-history") of His present human Lifetime—the great nineteenth-century Indian Realizers Sri Ramakrishna and Swami Vivekananda. Finally, Avatar Adi Da describes the series of profound transformational events that took place in the decades after His Divine Re-Awakening—each one a form of "Yogic death" for which there is no recorded precedent. Altogether, *The Knee of Listening* is the unparalleled history of how the Divine Conscious Light Incarnated in human Form, in order to grant everyone the possibility of Ultimate Divine Liberation, Freedom, and Happiness.

The Knee of Listening *is without a doubt the most profound Spiritual autobiography of all time.*

—ROGER SAVOIE, PhD
Philosopher; translator; author, *La Vipère et le Lion: La Voie radicale de la Spiritualité*

822 pp., **$24.95**
Also available in eBook edition!

MY "BRIGHT" WORD
by Avatar Adi Da Samraj

New edition of the classic Spiritual Discourses
originally published as *The Method of the Siddhas*

In these talks from the early years of His
Teaching-Work, Avatar Adi Da gives extraordinary
Instruction on the foundation of true Spiritual life,
covering topics such as the primary mechanism
that prevents the Realization of Truth, the means
to overcome this mechanism, and the true function
of the Spiritual Master in relation to the devotee.

*In modern language, this volume teaches the ancient all-time trans-egoic
truths. It transforms the student by paradox and by example. Consciousness,
understanding, and finally the awakened Self are the rewards. What more
can anyone want?*

—ELMER GREEN, PhD
Director Emeritus, Center for Applied Psychophysiology,
The Menninger Clinic

544 pp., **$24.95**

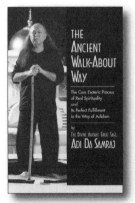

THE ANCIENT WALK-ABOUT WAY
The Core Esoteric Process of Real Spirituality and
Its Perfect Fulfillment in the Way of Adidam
by Avatar Adi Da Samraj

In this beautiful collection of essays, Avatar
Adi Da begins with a foundation consideration
of the purpose and principles of the ancient
tradition of devotional response to the living
Realizer; He then describes how to cultivate
life-conditions that allow the being to enact its
inherent devotional response to Living Truth;
and, finally, He describes the unique Signs and
Qualities of His Appearance and Offering, and of those who fully devotionally respond to Him.

Devotion to the Realizer is the ancient Way of true Spiritual life.
*Devotion to the Realizer is the "pre-civilization Way", which existed
before any recorded history, during a time when human beings were,
essentially, merely wandering all over the Earth. Devotion to the Realizer
has always been the fundamental Means of human Spirituality.*
—Avatar Adi Da Samraj

144 pp., **$12.95**
Also available in eBook edition!

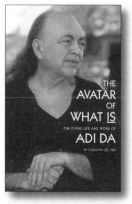

THE AVATAR OF WHAT IS

The Divine Life and Work of Adi Da
by Carolyn Lee, PhD

This biography presents a summary overview of Avatar Adi Da's Life and Work from His birth to 2007, the year before His physical passing. From the foretelling of His birth, through His years of "Learning humankind", to the more than thirty-five years of His unique Avataric Teaching and Blessing-Work, this is the extraordinary story of Adi Da's Divine Avataric Intervention in the world.

The Purpose of My bodily (human) Appearance here is the Divine Liberation of all of humankind—not merely the human beings of the East or the human beings of the West, but all human beings (and, indeed, all beings and things altogether).

—Avatar Adi Da Samraj

Avatar Adi Da's Divine Emergence marks a new chapter in epochal Spiritual History.

—RICHARD GROSSINGER
Author, *Planet Medicine, The Night Sky,* and *Embryogenesis*

152 pp., **$12.95**

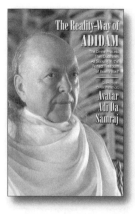

THE REALITY-WAY OF ADIDAM

The Divine Process that Outshines All Seeking in the Perfect Freedom of Reality Itself, Given by His Divine Presence, Avatar Adi Da Samraj
Written and compiled under the direct guidance of the Ruchira Sannyasin Order of Adidam Ruchiradam

A simple summary of the "radical" Way of life that Avatar Adi Da Samraj offers to all. Includes a discussion of the three foundation dimensions of Adidam Ruchiradam—"radical" devotion, right life, and "Perfect Knowledge"; a description of the Transcendental Spiritual process of Awakening in Avatar Adi Da's Eternal Blessing-Company; and a description of the unique nature of the Reality-Way of Adidam in the history of human religious and Spiritual endeavor.

255 pp., **$19.95**

Also available in eBook edition!

INTRODUCTORY COURSES
offered by teleconference through
THE LAUGHING MAN INSTITUTE
OF THE ADIDAM ACADEMY

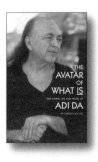

THE DA AVATAR

This four-week class is an introduction to the Life and Work of Adi Da Samraj including the examination of the uniqueness of Avatar Adi Da within the context of the Great Tradition of human wisdom and spirituality.

Required reading material:
The Avatar of What Is

THE REALITY-WAY OF ADIDAM

A four-week study of the three dimensions of the Reality-Way of Adidam: "Radical" devotion, right life, and "Perfect Knowledge", which simplify and clarify the foundation and practice of Adidam.

Required reading material:
The Reality-Way of Adidam

For more information and to register for courses, go to:

www.lmicourses.org

NOT-TWO IS PEACE
Expanded Third Edition
The Ordinary People's Way of Global Cooperative Order
by the World-Friend Adi Da

Not-Two Is Peace contains Adi Da's vital wisdom on the root of human conflict, the limits and errors of conventional religion and politics, and the necessity and means for global cooperation, tolerance, and peace via "the working presumption of prior unity". This book, which includes Adi Da's "radical" argument for the transcending of egoity, is essential study for anyone who is concerned about the state of global affairs. The expanded third edition (published early 2009) includes many new essays, and an entirely new section of core principles for the establishment of a "Global Cooperative Forum".

320 pp., **$14.95**

Also available in eBook edition!

EASY DEATH
Spiritual Wisdom on the Ultimate Transcending of Death and Everything Else
by Avatar Adi Da Samraj

This 2005 edition of *Easy Death* is thoroughly revised and updated with:
• Talks and essays by Avatar Adi Da on death and ultimate transcendence
• Accounts of profound Events of Yogic death in Avatar Adi Da's own Life
• Stories of His Blessing in the death transitions of His devotees

. . . [A]n exciting, stimulating, and thought-provoking book that adds immensely to the ever-increasing literature on the phenomena of life and death. But, more important, perhaps, it is a confirmation that a life filled with love instead of fear can lead to ultimately meaningful life and death. Thank you for this masterpiece.

—ELISABETH KÜBLER-ROSS, MD
Author, *On Death and Dying*

544 pp., **$24.95**

AUDIO-VISUAL

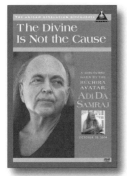

REALITY IS NOT WHAT YOU THINK

In this talk given to His devotees in April of 1995, Avatar Adi Da Samraj speaks about the limited nature of the "reality" that we commonly presume based on the "self"-contraction—and how to go beyond this presumption to Realize Reality as It actually Is.

Running time: 41 minutes.
CD, **$16.95**

THE DIVINE IS NOT THE CAUSE

From 2004 to 2006, Avatar Adi Da Samraj began a series of discourses that were broadcast live over the internet to all His devotees around the world. This DVD contains the discourse given by Adi Da Samraj in October of 2004, during which He is asked a series of questions about "self"-awareness, the nature of the ego, and how the "self"-contraction is caused. In response. He speaks of the effort to trace any experience or thought to its Source, and of Divine Reality as the True Condition of all things (not the "cause" of <u>any</u> thing).

Includes subtitles in English, Spanish, French, German, Dutch, Finnish, Polish, Czech, Chinese, Japanese, and Hebrew.

Running time: 72 minutes.
DVD, **$26.95**

THE DAWN HORSE PRESS

1-877-770-0772 (from within North America)
1-707-928-6653 (from outside North America)
www.dawnhorsepress.com

Find out more about
Avatar Adi Da Samraj
and His Reality-Way

■ Visit the ADIDAM™ website: **www.adidam.org**

■ Subscribe to the **AdiDaVideos** channel on YouTube

■ Or browse the Dawn Horse Press website for more books, audio, and video: **www.dawnhorsepress.com**

You can also contact one of our regional centers directly to find out how you can participate in courses and events nearest you:

AMERICAS	EUROPE-AFRICA	AUSTRALIA
12040 N. Seigler Rd.	Annendaalderweg 10	P.O. Box 244
Middletown, CA	6105 AT Maria Hoop	Kew 3101
95461 USA	The Netherlands	Victoria
correspondence@	**info@adidam.nl**	**info@adidamaustralia.org**
adidam.org	31 (0)20 468 1442	1800-234-326
1-707-928-4936		
	ASIA/PACIFIC	**INDIA**
THE UNITED	12 Seibel Road	F-168 Shree Love-Ananda Marg
KINGDOM	Henderson	Rampath, Shyam Nagar Extn.
and IRELAND	Auckland 0614	Jaipur - 302 019, India
uk@adidam.org	New Zealand	**info@adidam.in**
0845-330-1008	**auckland@**	91 (141) 2293080
	adidam.org	
	64-9-838-9114	